BOOKED

a TRAVELER'S GUIDE to LITERARY LOCATIONS AROUND the WORLD

RICHARD KREITNER

BLACK DOG
& LEVENTHAL
PUBLISHERS
NEW YORK

Black Dog & Leventhal Publishers
Hachette Book Group
1290 Avenue of the Americas
New York, NY 10104

www.hachettebookgroup.com
www.blackdogandleventhal.com

First Edition: April 2019

Black Dog & Leventhal Publishers is an imprint of Running Press, a division of Hachette Book Group.
The Black Dog & Leventhal Publishers name and logo are trademarks of Hachette Book Group, Inc.

The publisher is not responsible for websites (or their content) that are not owned by the publisher.

The Hachette Speakers Bureau provides a wide range of authors for speaking events. To find out more,
go to www.HachetteSpeakersBureau.com or call (866) 376-6591.

Photo credits can be found on page 222 and is an extension of the copyright page.

Print book interior design by Katie Benezra and Sheila Hart.

Library of Congress Cataloging-in-Publication Data

Names: Kreitner, Richard, 1990– author.
Title: Booked : a traveler's guide to literary locations around the world /
Richard Kreitner.
Description: New York, NY : Black Dog & Leventhal Publishers, 2019. |
Includes bibliographical references and index.
Identifiers: LCCN 2018045159| ISBN 9780316420877 (paper over board : alk.
paper) | ISBN 9780762465965 (ebook)
Subjects: LCSH: Literary landmarks—Guidebooks. | Travel—Guidebooks.
Classification: LCC PN164 .K74 2019 | DDC 809—dc23
LC record available at https://lccn.loc.gov/2018045159

Printed in China

1010

10 9 8 7 6 5 4 3 2 1

For my parents,
Robin and Al,
who taught me
to travel and to read.

CONTENTS

INTRODUCTION

I embarked on my first pilgrimage when I was twenty years old. In frigid, early-winter Montreal, where I was a third-year philosophy student, I struggled to explain to the girl I had just started dating my reasons for going on the trip. She was not convinced. Neither was I. And yet I felt I had to go—to "find" something, as the cliché goes, but even more, looking back, to lose something, too.

A week later, there I was: all alone atop a naked rocky peak as dawn lit up a quaint lakeside village far below, snowy mountains shimmering all around me. Shivering with cold, provisioned only with a bar of chocolate, and deliriously happy, I pulled out the book that had brought me there in the first place: a collection of William Wordsworth's poetry.

The village at my feet was Grasmere, in the English Lake District—where Wordsworth lived for fifteen years (before moving a few miles down the road), and where he is buried. Once, when he left town for a trip abroad, Wordsworth called Grasmere "the loveliest spot that man hath ever found." Looking down at a still, peaceful world cloaked in snowy silence, I fully agreed.

In the year since my first exposure to Wordsworth's work, I had read through his poetry over and over, especially *The Prelude*, his epic autobiographical poem about all the influences that had mysteriously, quietly, and unalterably shaped who and what he became. I was transfixed by its language and consoled by its assurances that nothing is really lost, everything counts, and all will be fine in the end. Like many twenty-year-olds, I thought what Wordsworth calls the "terrors, pains, and early miseries" of young adulthood would last forever. Who was I, and what would I become? Wordsworth promised the hidden workings of nature itself would see that these burning questions resolved themselves.

None of this, of course, explains why I went to Grasmere. I suppose I wanted to see the influences and impressions that had shaped Wordsworth—the peaks and valleys he explored as a boy, the meandering river that taught him constancy and change, the lakeside patch of thousands of daffodils he thought fondly of "in vacant or in pensive mood"—and, if only for a week, to make them my own.

The Vale of Grasmere in the English District.

Yet despite the exhilarating sunrise walk to the top of Helm Crag, the rocky peak jutting out over Grasmere, the terrors, pains, and miseries that had plagued me in Montreal seemed to have hitched a ride in my knapsack. Those days were a roller coaster of the highest highs and the lowest lows. As I sipped hand-pulled pints at the local pub, walked the fells (as locals call the district's barren hills), toured Wordsworth's famous Dove Cottage (which, incredibly to me, still had his two-hundred-year-old mirror), and sipped a few more pints, I struggled with the gnawing fear that I was somehow doing it wrong, that I wasn't communing as fully or as deeply as I should have been with Wordsworth, or Grasmere, or the fells.

I should have trusted Wordsworth more. In hindsight, I see the trip was a turning point. I came back different—a little calmer, stronger, more "worthy of myself," as *The Prelude* puts it.

In the decade since, I have spent much of my spare time making similar trips to places featured in some of my favorite books: poetry and prose, fictional or otherwise. Only now I am not alone. The girlfriend I left behind in Montreal—a fellow editor at the student newspaper—has since become my wife. She enjoys visiting authors' homes and other literary places at least as much as I do and has gamely consented to book-based excursions through the United States and around the world, from New Hampshire and Colorado to Poland and Greece. (Without her intelligence, indulgence, and Harry Potter expertise, this book, and everything else I have done, would have been impossible.)

Why *do* we search out places from literature? Most obviously it is to see how our mental image of it, shaped by the author's descriptions, matches up with reality. In our mind's eye, we map our conception of the place as it is described in the book onto what we see before us, and tally up how much is the same and how much is different, and of that which is different, how so.

Yet when we search out places from books, we are not simply looking for particular buildings or vistas or even atmospheres that made it into the work. There is something weirder and more magical going on. We want to see how the artist has transformed banal reality into the stuff of art. There is something even a little religious about it—thus the aptness of the word "pilgrimage."

When we travel to places featured in books we love, we are not only looking for how the place has impacted the book but how the book has impacted the place. After devouring a work that seems as if made only for us, it can be thrilling to see the fictional world so fully imagined in our minds recreated and saluted in this, the physical world—as in a statue of one of the characters (like that depicting Ignatius J. Reilly, from John Kennedy Toole's *A Confederacy of Dunces*, in New Orleans) or in a museum devoted to the author and his world (as in the National Steinbeck Center in Salinas, California). Such experiences extend the world of the book and allow us to live in it again, along with our fellow devotees.

In her 1956 essay, "Place in Fiction," the Mississippi-born writer Eudora Welty argued that literature is necessarily based in lived experience, tinged to a greater or lesser extent with local color. Novels are more than four-hundred-page postcards from a particular time and place—but they are that, too. "The truth is," Welty concluded, "fiction depends for its life on place."

According to Welty, the grounding of a story in a certain city or milieu is precisely what helps the reader to believe the story is "real"—whatever that means. As Welty wrote, "The moment the place in which the novel happens is accepted as true, through it will begin to glow, in a kind of recognizable glory, the feeling and thought that inhabited the novel in the author's head and animated the whole of his work." We suspend our disbelief—not only while reading the novel but even long after we have put it down.

The place where a story is set, then, is a sort of medium through which author and reader can trade thoughts, the setting for a meeting of the minds across all barriers of time and space and condition. It fosters one of the deepest connections possible. Among other things, literature is a form of cross-cultural communication. "Mutual understanding in the world being nearly always, as now, at low ebb, it is comforting to remember that it is through art that one country can nearly always speak reliably to another," Welty wrote. Armchair travel is not lazy, Welty argued, but noble—*liberal* in the truest and broadest sense of the word.

Literary tourism has seen a remarkable boom in recent years. According to the United States Department of Commerce, "cultural heritage" tourism has nearly doubled in the last decade, while tourism agencies have found that travelers who search out the "fictional underbelly" of a place tend to stay longer and spend more money. Unsurprisingly, literary tourism has also become a major source of study and investment, explored in academic journals and books from fields such as economics and the digital humanities, and in countless reports by regional planning associations.

Having a major new book take place in your town can utterly change the local economy: just ask the business leaders in Forks, Washington, the setting of Stephenie Meyer's Twilight trilogy for young adults. There, the local Chamber of Commerce bought a red Chevy truck to stand in for the one from the books. The city of Boston has launched a "Literary District," complete with special talks, guided tours, and app-driven guides that direct travelers to various fictional and cultural-historical destinations. There's also been an explosion of literary festivals devoted to local authors or even single works. "Bloomsday," the granddaddy of them all, celebrates June 16 as the day on which James Joyce set the action in *Ulysses*. From its first official celebration in Dublin in 1954, Bloomsday has since gone global.

Efforts to commemorate works of literature can, however, trigger a backlash if the book in question doesn't command wholehearted support from the local community. In Monroeville, Alabama, plans to massively build up tourism related to Harper Lee's *To Kill a Mockingbird* have run into criticisms that the project would turn the town into a "Disneyland for racists." A museum devoted to Sinclair Lewis in his hometown of Sauk Centre, Minnesota, recently closed, apparently undermined by lack of support in the area for a writer who poked fun at its backwardness and conformity. And activists in Boston and elsewhere have complained that designating particular neighborhoods as "literary districts" is a great way to ensure they become so expensive that no living, struggling writers can afford to live there.

Still, there is little threat that the mysterious alchemical process by which the base metal of reality is turned into the precious gold of art will come to a halt anytime soon. The literary destinations of the future, the homes of Nobel Prize winners yet to be born, the settings of world-renowned works yet to be written, may be in far-flung, out-of-the-way places that few outsiders have yet thought or even heard of. Who in Grasmere, in 1799, could have guessed that the handsome young poet who had just moved into the old abandoned inn at the edge of town would be the future poet laureate of the realm, and put their humble little hamlet on the map for centuries to come? Who in Gaborone, the capital of Botswana, in the early 1980s would have thought the local law professor would someday make their city world-famous with a blockbuster series of novels about a ladies' detective agency? Who near you today, as you read this, will tell the world what it was like to be a live human person in the first quarter of the twenty-first century, in the place where you now are? To ensure the job is done and done well, you may have to do it yourself.

From the Central Park carousel in J. D. Salinger's *The Catcher in the Rye* to Henry David Thoreau's cabin beside Walden Pond to Marcel Proust's enchanted bedroom at his aunt's home in the French country town of Illiers-Combray (renamed in homage to the author), readers can readily imagine—in exact, even eerie detail—the sights and sounds and smells of these places. But they can also be seen and heard and smelled in real life. The entries that follow describe some of the most famous and beloved places in literature—how they feature in the relevant work and what can be seen by visiting them. My hope is that this book will not only be read and passively enjoyed but also actively used in shaping your own literary pilgrimages, whether close to home or on the other side of the world. Mutual understanding being at a low ebb, as Eudora Welty noted so many decades ago, it is worth remembering the power of both art and travel to help us speak more reliably to one another, to make us more worthy of ourselves.

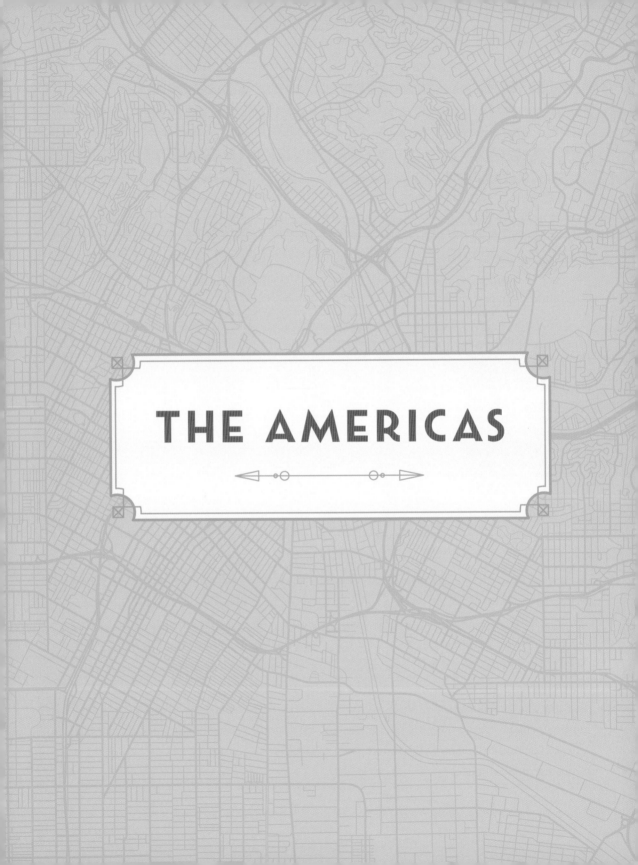

THE AMERICAS

The local water tower featured in *It*.

Odd Occurrences at the Standpipe in Derry

It, by Stephen King
Bangor, Maine

Stan Uris, the dweebiest, most logically minded, only Jewish member of the Losers Club in Stephen King's classic 1986 horror novel, *It*, likes to bird-watch. His favorite spot is a bench in the town park of Derry, near a shallow pool where birds often come to bathe. The bench is at the base of a hulking water tower called the Standpipe, which one character says is "as white as you imagine the robes of the archangels must be." People used to go up to the top for the sweeping views over the quiet town, but too many drownings meant the staircase had to be closed.

One day while he is bird-watching from the bench, Stan notices the Standpipe is

Stephen King's home in Bangor, Maine.

levitating off the ground. The door opens, though there is nobody else around. Stan approaches to take a closer look. He enters the dark tower and begins to tiptoe up the stairs. Suddenly he hears footsteps up ahead, sees weird shadows slinking around in the dark. The door at the bottom slams shut. He hears a voice call out on behalf of "the dead ones," those children who drowned in the tank. Stan, gripping his birding guide tight, starts to call out bird names at random to ward off whatever is in there with him. It works—the door opens to let him out.

Stan has had his first encounter with It, the shape-shifting homicidal entity from a universe not our own.

As Stephen King fans well know, the real-life inspiration for Derry is the author's hometown of Bangor, Maine, where his Gothic-style house stands behind an iron fence into which are carved fearsome, horrible shapes. The writer's fans flock from all around the world to see the house and to visit local places that inspired his fiction, like the Thomas Hill Standpipe, the inspiration for the water tank in *It*, built in 1897. King reportedly wrote most of the novel while sitting on the bench at the foot of the tower and across from the birdbath. The standpipe is only open to the public four days out of the year—once in each of the seasons. On other days one can sit on King's favorite bench and wait for the tower to levitate. If the door randomly opens, though, maybe think twice before venturing in.

WHERE TO VISIT

Thomas Hill Standpipe
Thomas Hill Road
Bangor, ME 04401

http://www.bangorwater.org

Sweet Hours in Amherst

The Poetry of Emily Dickinson
Amherst, Massachusetts

In 1830, Emily Dickinson was born in the ornate Federal-style house her grandfather had built two decades earlier, and she lived in that house for most of her life. It was there, at a small table in her large corner bedroom, shut away from the world, that Dickinson wrote her famously austere poems.

> *Sweet hours have perished here;*
> *This is a mighty room;*
> *Within its precincts hopes have played,—*
> *Now shadows in the tomb.*

Only a handful of her poems were published in her lifetime, but after Dickinson's death in 1886, her sister found a stack of pages locked away in a chest. Dickinson's house, and her brother's next to it, have been preserved as a museum, and visitors can even pay to rent her "mighty room" by the hour.

WHERE TO VISIT

Emily Dickinson Museum
280 Main Street
Amherst, MA 01002

http://www.emilydickinsonmuseum.org

The Mallard Family Finds a Home

Make Way for Ducklings, by Robert McCloskey
Boston, Massachusetts

Sometimes it's hard to figure where to put down roots and when to call a place home. That's true for bipeds of all kinds. At the opening of *Make Way for Ducklings,* the beloved children's book written and illustrated by Robert McCloskey and published in 1941, the Mallard family is looking for the ideal place to settle down. After scoping out the great sights of Boston from the air, Mr. and Mrs. Mallard decide to give the Public Garden a shot.

The place seems nice at first—leafy, watery—but it turns out to be too busy: Mr. Mallard is almost killed by a passing cyclist. They again take to the air and keep looking, finally picking a spot on the banks of the Charles River. There they hatch eight baby ducklings: Jack, Kack, Lack, Mack, Nack, Ouack, Pack, and Quack. Mr. Mallard—bored, perhaps, with the duties of domesticity—decides it's a good moment to take a little gander upriver and see what's there. He agrees to meet Mrs. Mallard back at the Public Garden in a week.

Nancy Schön's beloved 1987 sculpture of the Mallards.

Boston Public Garden, where the ducklings finally find a home.

Mrs. Mallard spends her time alone with the ducklings teaching them everything they'll need to know—how to fly, how to swim, how to dodge bicycles. When the day comes to meet up at the garden, Mrs. Mallard leads her ducklings across the river. Thanks to a little help from Michael, the friendly policeman who feeds the ducklings peanuts, the waterfowl safely waddle their way through Boston's busy streets to the Public Garden. Reunited, the family decides after all to make its home on the island in the garden's lagoon.

McCloskey got the idea for his award-winning book—which has sold more than two million copies and counting—while attending art school in Boston in the 1930s and spending a lot of his time in the Public Garden. Later, he worked on it in his Greenwich Village studio apartment, to which, one day, he brought a crate of live ducks to serve as models.

The city of Boston and the commonwealth of Massachusetts have wholly embraced *Make Way for Ducklings*. In 2000, over the objections of representatives from the city of Springfield, who thought the honor should go to a work by local author Dr. Seuss, McCloskey's book was voted the official children's book of Massachusetts. Every spring since 1978, the city has hosted an official Duckling Day in which young children and their parents dress as ducks and follow the Mallards' route through the streets.

The most famous tribute to the ducklings, of course, is the thirty-five-foot-long sculpture of Mrs. Mallard and her eight ducklings that the artist Nancy Schön installed in the Public Garden in 1987. One of the city's iconic tourist attractions, the sculpture is a favorite spot for families from Boston and around the world, a point of pride for the city. The ducks are often dressed in sports jerseys when local teams are in the playoffs.

Interestingly, the sculpture has also played a role in high-stakes Cold War diplomacy. In 1991, First Lady Barbara Bush gave her Russian counterpart, Raisa Gorbachev, a replica of the ducklings statue in a show of goodwill during the negotiations that led to the START treaty for military disarmament. The pieces of sculpture, including the cobblestones, and workers trained to install them were flown to Moscow by the United States Air Force. The replica can still be seen in the city's Novodevichy Park, along with a cemetery of Russian notables, a sixteenth-century convent, and, of course, plenty of live ducks. For some, despite all that has come between Russia and the United States in recent years, the message initially meant to be sent with the gift still holds true. "People are people everywhere," Tanya Malkova, a Moscow resident, told a Boston radio station in 2017. "So, the ducks in Boston and the ducks in Russia—they're the same as people are the same everywhere"—looking for a place to call home.

WHERE TO VISIT

Boston Public Garden
4 Charles Street
Boston, MA 02116
https://www.boston.gov/parks
/public-garden

A replica of Thoreau's cabin.

Life in the Woods Outside Concord

Walden, by Henry David Thoreau
Concord, Massachusetts

"I went to the woods because I wished to live deliberately," Henry David Thoreau writes early in *Walden*, his classic account of two years in a pond-front cabin on the edge of Concord, Massachusetts. "I wanted to live deep and suck out all the marrow of life, to live so sturdily and Spartan-like as to put to rout all that was not life, to cut a broad swath and shave close, to drive life into a corner, and reduce it to its lowest terms."

A former Harvard student and schoolteacher, a part-time philosopher and othertime pencil-maker, and at all times an avid naturalist, Thoreau decided, in the summer of 1845, to relocate to the shores of Walden Pond when his neighbor and mentor, the great sage Ralph Waldo Emerson, offered him some lakefront property for a writing retreat. Thoreau was working on his first book—the rambling travelogue, *A Week on the Concord and Merrimack Rivers*—and needed some time away from it all. He built a one-room cabin, largely from discarded planks, at a spot with a view of a nearby cove. From July 1845 to September 1847, Thoreau lived in the cabin a mile from his nearest neighbor—reading, writing, maintaining a small garden, absorbing the teachings of nature, reducing life to its barest terms.

The pond is, in fact, a kettle lake formed by a chunk of ice left by a retreating glacier.

After his return to Concord, Thoreau worked on his book about "Life in the Woods," as his subtitle had it. Published in 1854, the strange, unclassifiable work sold modestly at first. Over time, however, it became a quintessential national text. "In one book," the poet Robert Frost once observed, "he surpasses everything we have had in America."

The cabin Thoreau lived in was broken down and removed not long after he vacated the property, and the precise location of it was forgotten—a cairn of stones placed by latter-day admirers marked only a rough approximation. In 1945, exactly a century after Thoreau took up residence at Walden, an amateur archaeologist unearthed the original hearthstone. The site is now indicated by standing stones and a small plaque.

In the twentieth century, Emerson's descendants deeded the property to the state, and in the 1970s, after several battles to fight development at the pond (including one proposal that would have leveled much of the woods for a parking lot), a state park opened. More land in the area was preserved in 1990, when Don Henley of The Eagles, inspired by his reading of Thoreau in college, formed the Walden Woods Project. The project's nearby Thoreau Institute promotes environmental awareness and the ideas and writings of its namesake.

The transcendentalist used his time at Walden Pond as an experiment in living.

Walden Pond itself is open for swimming, fishing, and canoeing in warm weather, and for cross-country skiing, and snowshoeing in the cold. In truth, it's not even necessary to go all the way to Massachusetts for a sense of what Thoreau found so appealing about the simplicities of cabin life. The website Walden Labs offers information about how to build your own replica of Thoreau's dwelling—without electricity or plumbing, mind you—and for roughly the same amount he doled out, less than $1,000 in today's dollars.

Today, visitors continue to arrive from all over the world to get a glimpse of what many consider the birthplace of the environmental movement. There are two replicas of Thoreau's cabin that can be visited in Concord, one near the parking lots at Walden Pond (constructed in the 1970s with cutting-edge porous-asphalt technology) and the other on the grounds of the Concord Museum, across the street from Emerson's house. The museum also boasts Thoreau's original bed, chair, and desk. Between the two sites is a lovely 1.7-mile walking path, the Emerson-Thoreau Amble, which winds through forests and fields for a brief taste of the ever-enchanting (and ever-changing) New England landscape.

"A lake is the landscape's most beautiful and expressive feature," Thoreau wrote in one chapter of *Walden*. "It is earth's eye; looking into which the beholder measures the depth of his own nature."

WHERE TO VISIT

Walden Pond State Reservation
915 Walden Street
Concord, MA 01742

https://www.mass.gov/locations
/walden-pond-state-reservation

Concord Museum
200 Lexington Road
Concord, MA 01742

http://www.concordmuseum.org

The Thoreau Institute
44 Baker Farm Road
Lincoln, MA 01773

https://www.walden.org

Finding Freedom in 1840s New Bedford

Moby-Dick, by Herman Melville and
Narrative of the Life of Frederick Douglass
New Bedford, Massachusetts

In the early 1840s, New Bedford, Massachusetts, looked like a forest of masts and sounded like a Babel of foreign tongues. It was the whaling capital of the world, and one of the richest towns in New England. Every day it sent and received ships that prowled the world's seas for the precious whale blubber used to make such products as lamp oil, candles, and fertilizer. Like many dynamic port cities, it boasted a diverse array of inhabitants.

With such a colorful cast of characters coming and going all at once, out to sea and back to land, New Bedford was suffused with a spirit of adventure, liberty, and come-as-you-are hospitality. It's no coincidence, then, that two of the most exceptional American writers of the nineteenth century, though they didn't know each other and never would, found themselves in New Bedford around the same time, and with the same goal: Both were trying to get away.

Herman Melville's name will forever be attached to New Bedford, where, without

Thanks to the whaling industry, the New Bedford of the 1840s was a uniquely diverse and liberty-loving city.

The Seamen's Bethel, scene of perhaps the most famous sermon in literature.

any other job prospects, he stopped briefly in late 1840 before shipping out on his first whaling voyage. Melville would immortalize the town's grimy but spirited atmosphere in the early scenes of *Moby-Dick*, when the narrator, Ishmael, arrives from New York and has trouble finding a place to stay. "Such dreary streets! blocks of blackness, not houses, on either hand, and here and there a candle, like a candle moving about in a tomb," Melville wrote. After wandering through town, Ishmael finds an inn, but he has to sleep beside the good-natured, harpoon-bearing cannibal Queequeg. The next morning, before heading out, Ishmael takes in a sermon at the Whalemen's Chapel, where

plaques on the wall name men lost at sea. The preacher climbs a rope ladder into his pulpit, shaped like the bow of a ship, and lectures the sailors about the biblical story of Jonah and the whale: "And here, shipmates, is true and faithful repentance; not clamorous for pardon, but grateful for punishment."

The Whalemen's Chapel in *Moby-Dick* was based on a real church called the Seamen's Bethel. It still exists, as part of the New Bedford Whaling National Historical Park. Yet there's one notable difference between how it looks today and how it looked in Melville's time: Now there really is a ship-shaped pulpit like the one Melville made up for the novel, a striking instance of life imitating art.

The Nathan and Mary Johnson House, where Frederick Douglass first stayed while in New Bedford.

Though the slave-born Frederick Bailey had far more urgent reasons than Melville for trying to escape his past life, he, too, was drawn to the freedom-friendly atmosphere of New Bedford in the early 1840s. The democratic equality that prevailed on the whaling ships held true onshore as well in the town one scholar has called "the fugitive's Gibraltar." A major stop on the Underground Railroad, New Bedford had the largest percentage of black residents anywhere in the Northeast, and many were known to be escaped slaves. After fleeing Maryland by railcar in 1838, and arriving in New York by ship, Bailey married Anna Murray, a free black woman who had helped him escape. From there they sailed to Newport, and then continued on to New Bedford, where the couple was taken in by friendly abolitionists. "We now began to feel a degree of safety," he recalled in his autobiographical *Narrative*, "and to prepare ourselves for the duties and responsibilities of a life of freedom." It was around the breakfast table the morning after their arrival that Frederick and Anna decided to change their last name to Douglass. It was suggested by one of their hosts, who took it from the name of a warrior in "The Lady of the Lake," a poem by Sir Walter Scott.

Douglass's first move was to visit the wharves at the harbor, where he was astounded by the impressive array of ships and the fabulous displays of prosperity— surprising to him, for he had inadvertently "imbibed the notion" that there could be no wealth without slaves. He left the wharves and walked around town, "gazing with wonder and admiration at the splendid churches, beautiful dwellings, and finely-cultivated gardens." Yet, Douglass went on, "the most astonishing as well as the most interesting thing to me was the condition of the colored people, a great many of whom, like myself,

had escaped thither as a refuge from the hunters of men. I found many, who had not been seven years out of their chains, living in finer houses, and evidently enjoying more of the comforts of life, than the average of slaveholders in Maryland."

It was his first glimpse of freedom, and Douglass found the possibilities intoxicating. He took a job at the docks—the same ones Melville described in *Moby-Dick*—and felt great joy for the first time in laboring as a free man. "It was a happy moment, the rapture of which can be understood only by those who have been slaves," he recalled. "It was the first work, the reward of which was to be entirely my own."

A few months after settling in New Bedford, Douglass was introduced to the fiery Boston abolitionist William Lloyd Garrison's newspaper, *The Liberator*, which Douglass said "became my meat and my drink," and shortly after that he heard Garrison speak "his mighty words, mighty in truth." It didn't take long for Douglass's own abilities to come to Garrison's attention, and he became famous on both sides of the Atlantic for his antislavery advocacy. Later, he moved to Rochester, New York. But it was New Bedford that had given Douglass his start, New Bedford that had shown him what a more free and equal society looked like, what a free man could do.

There's nothing in the record to suggest

that Douglass and Melville encountered each other in New Bedford, though the great abolitionist was certainly in town when the author of *Moby-Dick* passed through. But as Douglass's descriptions of the city's waterfront indicate, they are perhaps not altogether absent in one another's works. While traipsing around New Bedford on the night of his arrival, Ishmael, seeking a place to rest, walks into a building with an open door and a loud voice shouting within: "A hundred black faces turned round in their rows to peer; and beyond, a black Angel of Doom was beating a book in a pulpit. It was a negro church; and the preacher's text was about the blackness of darkness, and the weeping and wailing and teeth-gnashing there." Realizing his mistake, Ishmael walks out.

WHERE TO VISIT

Seamen's Bethel
15 Johnny Cake Hill
New Bedford, MA 02740

http://www.seamensbethel.org

Nathan and Mary Johnson House
21 Seventh Street
New Bedford, MA 02740

http://www.nps.gov/nr/travel/underground/ma6.htm

New Bedford Whaling National Historical Park
33 William Street
New Bedford, MA 02740

http://www.nps.gov/nebe/index.htm

Mystical Sunsets over Providence

The Fiction of H. P. Lovecraft
Providence, Rhode Island

Imprisoned monsters, interstellar demons, underwater cities, and murderous fungi: In dozens of short stories and hundreds of poems, H. P. Lovecraft imagined a whole strange universe. Largely ignored before his death in 1937 at the age of forty-six—he earned a paltry living writing for pulp magazines like *Weird Tales* and doing bits of hack work, and died broke—Lovecraft's legendary evocations of the Cthulhu Mythos, as some call his fictional universe, have earned him posthumous fame and widespread admiration that continue to grow. Throughout the world, he is considered the godfather of modern science-fiction and horror writing. In his hometown, too, Lovecraft has become something of a hero.

Howard Phillips Lovecraft was born in Providence, Rhode Island, and lived in the city his whole life—except for a brief (and sorrowful) spell in Brooklyn shortly after his marriage. There are still several places around Providence connected with the writer; most of them are easily accessible in a brief self-guided tour. The house where he was born on Angell Street, which he hoped one day to have enough money to purchase, was torn down in 1961 (a stone marker relates the Lovecraft connection). Just down the block is the house (at 598 Angell) where he lived for twenty years as he first began honing his craft. After his return to Providence from Brooklyn, Lovecraft moved into 10 Barnes Street, where he and his wife lived in "a fine large ground-floor room" from 1926 to 1933. This was probably the most fruitful period of his career; here he churned out "The Call of Cthulhu," the story that first introduced readers to the winged, octopus-shaped monster, and *The Shadow over Innsmouth* (1936), the only Lovecraft story published as a book during his lifetime.

Lovecraft's final residence in Providence was the upper floor of a "venerable dwelling" on College Street, a Georgian structure, built in 1825, which displayed all the "earmarks of early Nineteenth Century workmanship," as Lovecraft wrote—"a cozy and fascinating place, in a little garden oasis of village-like antiquity." The house had a

Lovecraft adored Providence, especially the view of the city from Prospect Terrace Park.

The horror writer often used the private library at the Providence Athenaeum.

"haunting vista," for it was close to Prospect Terrace Park and its statue of Providence founder Roger Williams. Lovecraft loved walking there and taking in the "mystical sunsets" over the city. In fact, though much of his work focused on bizarre, otherworldly phenomena, Lovecraft had a particular knack for describing this quintessential Providence view. In *The Case of Charles Dexter Ward*—his longest story, not published until after his death—Lovecraft describes "the great westward sea of hazy roofs and domes and steeples and far hills… all violent and mystic against a fevered, apocalyptic sunset of reds and golds and purples and curious greens."

While living in the College Street home,

Lovecraft also wrote "The Haunter of the Dark," his last story, in which the main character, a writer named Robert Blake, lives in that home and can see a large, abandoned church rumored to have a strange association with murder and the occult.

After Lovecraft's death, his home was moved to accommodate Brown University's expansion. It no longer boasts the views of those "mystical sunsets," but it's still a pilgrimage place for Lovecraft's global legion of fans. Off and on since the early 1990s the city has played host to a NecronomiCon festival in Lovecraft's honor. In 2015, on the 125th anniversary of his birth, two thousand people attended the convention. The following year brought the first annual

Lovecraft Film Festival, which also included author-themed walking tours. Downtown, in the Providence Arcade, the Lovecraft Arts & Sciences store sells books by the local hero and other works inspired by him. It's also a gathering place for those interested in tracking down Lovecraft-related sites in Providence.

Elsewhere in the history-infused city, the Providence Athenaeum, a beautiful library (private, but open to visitors) where he used to do research, has a bust of the author, and the John Hay Library at Brown University, right next to the original College Street location of his last home, boasts Lovecraft manuscripts, letters, and other personal effects, as well as a few oddities he would have found fascinating, like books bound in human skin. A plaque put up in 1990, the centennial of his birth, quotes from a poem in the collection of Lovecraft's sonnets known as *Fungi from Yuggoth*:

I never can be tied to raw, new things,
For I first saw the light in an old town,
Where from my window huddled roofs
*   sloped down*
To a quaint harbour rich with visionings.

Streets with carved doorways where the
*   sunset beams*
Flooded old fanlights and small win-
*   dow-panes,*

And Georgian steeples topped with
*   gilded vanes—*
These were the sights that shaped my
*   childhood dreams.*

H. P. Lovecraft is buried in his family plot in the city's Swan Point Cemetery, near the Seekonk River. People come from all over the world to leave various items—pens, pennies, figurines, notes with eerie messages, esoteric drawings. Lovecraft was so poor when he died that his survivors couldn't even afford to erect a monument in his memory. Only years later did his admirers pool funds to set one up. It features an apt quote from a letter of his: "I am Providence."

WHERE TO VISIT

H. P. Lovecraft's last home (private)
65 Prospect Street
Providence, RI 02906

Providence Athenaeum
251 Benefit Street
Providence, RI 02903
https://providenceathenaeum.org

John Hay Library
20 Prospect Street
Providence, RI 02912
https://library.brown.edu/hay/

At the end of the novel, Holden takes his kid sister for a ride on the carousel.

Holden Caulfield's Central Park

The Catcher in the Rye, by J. D. Salinger
Manhattan, New York

After flunking out of the all-boys boarding school Pencey Prep, Holden Caulfield, the hilariously cynical, precocious, and ever-curious sixteen-year-old narrator of J. D. Salinger's iconic 1951 novel, *The Catcher in the Rye*, decides to go back home to New York City a few days earlier than expected.

Riding in a taxi on the way to the hotel where he plans to stay before revealing the truth to his wealthy parents, a random thought pops into Holden's head. He promptly puts it to the cab driver.

"You know those ducks in that lagoon right near Central Park South? That little lake?" he asks. "By any chance, do you happen to know where they go, the ducks, when it gets all frozen over? Do you happen to know, by any chance?"

Unsurprisingly, the cab driver has no idea. "What're ya tryna do, bud? Kid me?" he asks.

Holden knows the question is random and may not even be sure why he cares, but in the course of the novel the ducks become a symbol of Holden's more general predicament. The ducks' disappearance in the winter represents Holden's deepest fears—of responsibility, of mortality, of change.

Later, Holden visits the Central Park pond to find the answer for himself. Though he has "the most terrific trouble finding that lagoon," he eventually stumbles upon it—only to discover, however, that there isn't "a single duck." They're gone.

Newly landscaped with an island habitat for birds and turtles, the lagoon near the southern entrance to Central Park is still there. Sometimes the ducks do remain there, even in winter.

A few miles north, on another side of the park, there's another New York landmark mentioned in *Catcher* as a symbol of Holden's fear of change. Standing in front of the American Museum of Natural History, Holden recalls fond childhood memories of visiting the diorama exhibits, especially one that featured Native Americans "rubbing sticks together to make a fire, and a squaw weaving a blanket." Although dirty-minded Holden is partly fascinated because he could "see the squaw's bosom and all," what amazes him most is the fact that the exhibits never changed: "Everything always stayed right where it was. Nobody'd move… Nobody'd be different. The only thing that would be different would be you." The diorama is still on display, unchanged.

Back in the park, there's one more real-life testament to the story of Holden's agonizing march to breakdown and, perhaps, maturity. It's the location of the final scene of the novel: the Central Park Carousel.

Holden Caulfield wonders where the ducks go when the pond in Central Park freezes over in winter.

After finally going home, Holden meets with his younger sister, Phoebe. Together, the two head into the Central Park Zoo and check out the sea lions. Then they go to the carousel, where Holden watches as Phoebe makes her way around the circle and tries to grab the golden ring. Although he's "afraid she'd fall off the goddamn horse" in the attempt, Holden decides not to intervene. He tells us, "the thing with kids is, if they want to grab for the gold ring, you have to let them do it…if they fall off, they fall off." Only then does Holden finally accept that everyone has to make mistakes, accept change, and grow up.

Today's Central Park Carousel isn't the same one that Phoebe rode, and the golden rings have gone out of fashion—our litigious society, apparently, hasn't quite learned the lesson Holden did—but it's still a place *Catcher* fans visit to commune with Holden's spirit.

WHERE TO VISIT

American Museum of Natural History
Central Park West & 79th Street
New York, NY 10024
https://www.amnh.org

Central Park Carousel
1802 65th Street Transverse
New York, NY 10065
https://www.centralpark.com/things-to-do
/attractions/carousel/

An Aching Affection for Newark

The Novels of Philip Roth
Newark, New Jersey

"I felt a deep knowledge of Newark, an attachment so rooted that it could not help but branch out into affection," Neil Klugman, the protagonist of Philip Roth's breakout 1959 novella, *Goodbye, Columbus*, declares.

Like Klugman, the late author had a deep affection for his hometown of Newark, New Jersey, just a train ride (and a world) away from New York City, as his highly autobiographical works reveal. Many of them centered on the same place: the Newark of Roth's childhood in the 1930s and 1940s—specifically, in what was then the Jewish part of Newark, Weequahic.

In *Goodbye, Columbus*, Neil Klugman is a hapless youth who spends his summers working in the Newark Public Library, a turn-of-the-century limestone Italian Renaissance–style structure on Washington

The Newark Public Library, where Neil Klugman works in *Goodbye, Columbus.*

Street, still much the same as it was in Roth's day. Close by is Washington Park, where one morning before work, Neil decides to take a stroll. The park smells "of trees, night, and dog leavings; and there was a faint damp smell too, indicating that the huge rhino of a water cleaner had passed by already, soaking and whisking the downtown streets." Behind the library is the Newark Museum (recently renovated). "I could see it without even looking," Neil notes. "Two oriental vases in front like spittoons for a rajah, and next to it the little annex to which we had traveled on special buses as schoolchildren."

Another of Roth's works set in Newark is *Portnoy's Complaint* (1969), his most famous—and outrageous—book, about a Jewish boy who cannot control his sexual urges. Portnoy attends Weequahic High School, at the time mostly Jewish, where he and his friends cheer after sports events:

> *Ikey, Mikey, Jake and Sam,*
> *We're the boys who eat no ham,*
> *We play football, we play soccer—*
> *And we keep matzohs in our locker!*
> *Aye, aye, aye, Weequahic High!*

Portnoy spends much of his time playing softball in the fields off Chancellor Avenue, in games where he presents himself as a "perfect joining of clown and competitor, kibitzing wiseguy and dangerous long-ball hitter."

Intersecting with Chancellor Avenue is Summit Avenue, the street of Roth's childhood. The narrator of *The Plot Against America* (2004), also named Philip Roth, describes it as "tinged with the bright after-storm light…agleam with life." The real Roth's birthplace at 81 Summit Avenue now has a plaque honoring the author.

Not far away, the narrator mentions, is "grassy, wooded Weequahic Park…a land-scaped three hundred acres whose boating lake, golf course, and harness-racing track separated the Weequahic section from the industrial plants and shipping terminals lining Route 27 and the Pennsylvania Railroad viaduct east of that and the burgeoning airport east of that and the very edge of America east of that."

Weequahic High School, where Roth graduated in 1950.

Other landmarks mentioned in the novel can still be seen today, though mere ghosts of a more glorious past: the Riviera Hotel, where the narrator's "mother and father had spent their wedding night," and Temple B'nai Abraham, "the great oval fortress built to serve the city's Jewish rich and no less foreign to me than if it had been the Vatican." (The congregation moved to nearby Livingston in 1973, but the fortress itself still stands.)

In *I Married a Communist* (1998), Roth's alter ego Nathan Zuckerman tells the story of Ira Ringold, an idealistic political radical whose life is turned upside down in McCarthy-era America when his ex-wife writes an exposé that leaves him blacklisted. Writing about the columned Essex County Courthouse in the poorer part of Newark, Nathan describes the way Ira would ask people what they thought about changing "the crappy system and the damn problem of ignorant cruelty" that he believed was ruining society. Nathan goes on to compare his do-gooding friend to Abraham Lincoln, whose statue sits in front of the courthouse.

The not-so-gradual transition of Newark from a more or less decent place to grow up to its more recent association with rampant violence and disinvestment is considered in one of Roth's greatest works, *American Pastoral* (1997). In the novel, Seymour "the Swede" Levov (a former all-star athlete at Weequahic High) calls Newark a place that

Roth's childhood home on Summit Avenue, in Newark's old Jewish neighborhood.

once "manufactured everything" but has since turned into "the car theft capital of the world." As he sits at his desk in Newark, the Swede discusses what he sees around him: "Springfield Avenue in flames, South Orange Avenue in flames, Bergen Street under attack, sirens going off, weapons firing… looting crowds crazed in the streets."

The Newark of Roth's childhood might be a remnant of a bygone age, but it still lives on in his fiction and in the many places that, while perhaps changed, are still standing. Not long before his death in 2018, Roth announced that he was donating his collection of four thousand books to the Newark Public Library, a testament to the crucial place Newark held in his heart as long as he lived—an attachment so deeply rooted it branched out into affection.

WHERE TO VISIT

Weequahic Park
Elizabeth Avenue & Meeker Avenue
Newark, NJ 07112

https://www.essexcountyparks.org/parks
/weequahic-park

Newark Public Library
5 Washington Street
Newark, NJ 07101

https://npl.org

Philip Roth's childhood home (private)
81 Summit Avenue
Newark, NJ 07112

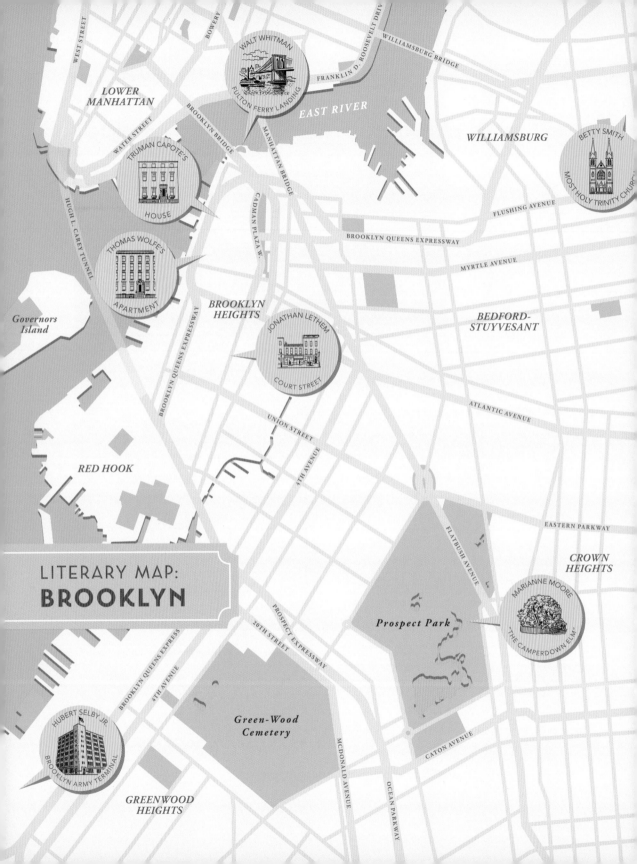

Literary Brooklyn

Walt Whitman, Betty Smith, Truman Capote, Marianne Moore, Thomas Wolfe, Alfred Kazin, Paule Marshall, Hubert Selby Jr., Jonathan Lethem

These days, no place on the globe is as much associated with the manufacture of literature as Brooklyn, New York, where this very book, in fact, was written. The clichés are all true: the hunched-over wannabe-novelist in every café, the insufferable (and unmissable) book-world parties. (One recent author went out of his way to mention on his book's cover jacket that he *didn't* live in the borough.) But there is also a lot more to literary Brooklyn than might first meet the eye; namely, the millions of nonwriterly residents in the city's most populous borough—too busy raising kids, working two or three jobs, trying to improve their families' lives to worry about who got the latest seven-figure advance and what the privileged editors of one prestigious journal said about those of

Only the dead know Brooklyn: The view looking north and west over the borough, toward Manhattan.

another. What's truly literary about Brooklyn isn't the sheer density of writers and editors who live there but the sheer amount of lives being lived, from Canarsie to Bay Ridge, DUMBO to Bushwick, all the freaking time. "It'd take a guy a lifetime to know Brooklyn t'roo an' t'roo," says the narrator of Thomas Wolfe's classic 1935 short story "Only the Dead Know Brooklyn." "An' even den, yuh wouldn't know it all." The same is true of Brooklyn-based literature. Here, however, is a start.

The godfather of Brooklyn letters, of course, is **Walt Whitman**. Born on Long Island, he lived in the then-independent city during the formative years of his adult life, when he worked as the editor of the *Brooklyn Eagle*, based on Fulton Street. Often, the journalist would end the day by walking down to the East River and boarding a ferry to Manhattan, where he spent his evenings drinking in bohemian Greenwich Village dive bars and carousing late into the night.

Whitman name-checked many Brooklyn places in his poetry and even more in his journalism, but perhaps the Kings County location most associated with the barbaric yawper isn't in Brooklyn proper at all, but on that ferry between the Fulton slip and the Manhattan docks. In "Crossing Brooklyn Ferry," a poem included in the first 1855 edition of *Leaves of Grass* and repeatedly altered in subsequent versions, Whitman expresses his love for the teeming cacophony on the boat, the faces and noises and smells. "Crowds of men and women attired in the usual costumes, how curious you are to me!" he sings. While many then bemoaned (as they do now) the sheer mass of humanity that had to be reckoned with on public transit, Whitman rejoiced in what it revealed about the interconnectedness of human beings and indeed all things. The experience of riding the ferry opened his mind to a sense of cosmic timelessness, the universality of experiences good and bad and neither and both: the ups and downs, the rushes of contradictory emotions, the triumphs and imperfections, the regrets and the hopes. These insights made him think that fifty or a hundred years later people would still be experiencing the same thing. In the poem he reaches out to Brooklynites of the future:

> I am with you, you men and women of a
>   generation, or ever so many generations
>   hence,
> Just as you feel when you look on the river
>   and sky, so I felt,
> Just as any of you is one of a living crowd,
>   I was one of a crowd,
> Just as you are refresh'd by the gladness of the
>   river and the bright flow, I was refresh'd,

Just as you stand and lean on the rail, yet
    hurry with the swift current, I stood yet
    was hurried,
Just as you look on the numberless masts of
    ships and the thick-stemm'd pipes of
    steamboats, I look'd.

Of course, the East River is somewhat less clogged with steamboats these days—the technology that seemed so new and exciting in Whitman's day has long since been superseded. Perhaps, then, nothing is quite as timeless as "Crossing Brooklyn Ferry" would have us believe. After all, within Whitman's own lifetime—though after he had left Brooklyn, first for Washington and then for the bucolic pastures (seriously!) of Camden, New Jersey—the opening of the majestic Brooklyn Bridge rendered the old Fulton Ferry irrelevant literally overnight; after years of decline, it finally ceased operations in 1924.

In recent years, however, ferries have once again begun braving the river's tide-swelled waves. In 2011, the new East River Ferry began operating with seven stops in Brooklyn, Manhattan, and Queens, including a new dock at the foot of Fulton Street; within a few years the network expanded further to include seventeen piers. Once again riders can be among the living crowd, can be refreshed by the gladness of the river, can lean on the rail and be hurried along. Set

up to abate crowding on the city's subways and buses, the ferries have seen ridership levels soar far beyond official projections. (Oddly enough, the beards and mustaches on some passengers even add to the effect of traveling back in time.) Not far from the ferry slip in Brooklyn Bridge Park is an outpost of the Whitman-inspired ice-cream joint Ample Hills Creamery, with the immortal words from "Crossing Brooklyn Ferry" painted on the wall:

I TOO LIVED, BROOKLYN
    OF AMPLE HILLS WAS MINE.

WHERE TO VISIT

Fulton Ferry Landing
Brooklyn Bridge Park
334 Furman Street
Brooklyn, NY 11201
https://www.brooklynbridgepark.org
/park/fulton-ferry-landing

Betty Smith's *A Tree Grows in Brooklyn* (1943) is a coming-of-age tale largely set in the Nolan family's tenements in East Williamsburg, in 1912. (They live first on Bogart Street, then Lorimer, and finally Grand.) Eleven-year-old Francie Nolan is a young girl born to poor parents. "There was no bathroom and the toilet was in the hall and shared by two

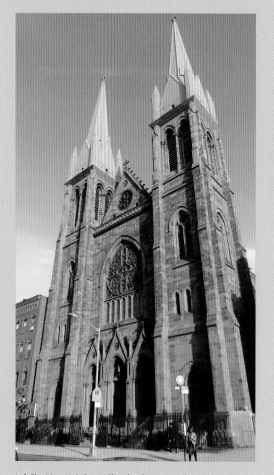

Left: The Most Holy Trinity Church, where many German immigrants worshipped at the turn of the twentieth century, is described in the novel as the borough's "most beautiful" house of worship. Right: The Williamsburg Bridge.

families," Smith writes of one apartment. She knew what she was talking about, having been born to a working-class family in the neighborhood in 1896.

The book is full of rich descriptions of Williamsburg, as when Francie and her brother, Neeley, run chores on Manhattan Avenue, "past Maujer, Ten Eyck, Stagg to Scholes Street. Beautiful names for ugly streets. From each side street hordes of little ragamuffins emerged to swell the main tide." Many of the area's tenements have since been replaced by public housing projects where young working-class children face the same difficulties the Nolan family had. Elsewhere in the book Francie attends mass at what she considers "the most beautiful church in Brooklyn…It was made of old gray stone and had twin spires that rose cleanly into the sky, high above the tallest tenements." The church

is likely the still-standing Most Holy Trinity Church, just a few blocks away at 138 Montrose Avenue, where Smith herself was baptized.

Near the end of the novel, Francie and Neeley are looking out on the town from their roof. "There's no other place like it," Francie says with wonder. "Like what?" Neeley asks. "Brooklyn!" Francie answers. "It's a magic city and it isn't real."

WHERE TO VISIT

Most Holy Trinity Church
138 Montrose Avenue
Brooklyn, NY 11206

https://mostholytrinity-brooklyn.org

It might seem inevitable that the endless, leaf-lined streets of Brooklyn, dotted with well-preserved parks, would attract novelists, journalists, and poets. But Brooklyn wasn't always so serene. In the mid-twentieth century, **Truman Capote** felt he had to explain why he had decided to take up residence in the benighted borough—first in a humble apartment in Clinton Hill and then in a majestic 1839 mansion in Brooklyn Heights.

"I live in Brooklyn. By Choice," Capote famously wrote in the opening sentence of "A House on the Heights," a 1959 essay. "Those ignorant of its allures are entitled to wonder why. For, taken as a whole, it is an uninviting community…Yet, in the greenless grime-gray, oases do occur, splendid contradictions, hearty echoes of healthier days." Brooklyn Heights was an example, with its "sea gull's view of the Manhattan and Brooklyn bridges, of lower Manhattan's tall dazzle and the ship-lane waters, breeding river to bay to ocean, that encircle and seethe past posturing Miss Liberty." The house in which Capote kept his apartment sold a few years ago for $12 million.

WHERE TO VISIT

Truman Capote's former house (private)
70 Willow Street
Brooklyn, NY 11201

The house on Willow Street in Brooklyn Heights where Truman Capote rented a few rooms in the basement from 1955 to 1965.

In 1872, just a few years after Prospect Park opened to the public, a florist in the East New York neighborhood gifted the city a very special tree. It was a Camperdown Elm, one of the few in the world descended from the original of the species, which had been developed by an experimental arborist in Scotland some forty years earlier. The tree cannot reproduce itself; its knobby limbs, drooping to the ground, need lots of support and sustenance to survive. When the Camperdown Elm was planted in Prospect Park, near the Boathouse, it was rooted on a little hillock so as to give the heavy, weeping arms a better chance of clearing the ground.

By the 1960s, the tree was neglected and at serious risk of dying. A gaping hole in its trunk had been shoddily filled with concrete and rats had taken up residence in its wood. Rescue came in a peculiarly literary form. In 1965, **Marianne Moore**, a longtime resident of Brooklyn (she lived for nearly forty years at 260 Cumberland Street near Fort Greene Park), was elected president of the Greensward Foundation, a public advocacy group set up to support New York's neglected parks. She

The Camperdown Elm in Prospect Park.

became fascinated by the tree and what its helplessness signified about the interconnectedness of all living things (note the Whitman connection). In 1967, at almost eighty years old, she wrote a poem, "The Camperdown Elm," about what would be required to save the endangered tree:

Props are needed and tree-food.
It is still leafing;
still there. Mortal though.
We must save it. It is
our crowning curio.

Save it the city did. Moore's poem, which was published in the *New Yorker*, sparked a public campaign to buttress the tree with wooden crutches and a complicated array of cables and rods that help keep it alive today, along with a low black fence that keeps the public away. A century and a half later it is still leafing, still there. In 2017, a restaurant opened just a few blocks away, in Park Slope, named for the aged arboreal survivor.

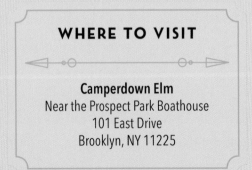

WHERE TO VISIT

Camperdown Elm
Near the Prospect Park Boathouse
101 East Drive
Brooklyn, NY 11225

After his groundbreaking first novel *Look Homeward, Angel*, set in his hometown of Asheville, North Carolina, was published to rave reviews in 1929, **Thomas Wolfe** became one of the most famous writers in America. Fans sent him letters by the satchel and even tracked him down, while the Manhattan literati feted him as the next big thing. Wolfe didn't enjoy the adulation, however; he felt alienated from the New York literary scene, even a little intimidated. After a ten-month trip to Europe, he wanted to find a place he could settle down to write and reconnect with the down-to-earth "real" America he had known while growing up.

He decided to rent a room in "the quaint old town of Brooklyn." It was just far enough from Manhattan to give him much-needed isolation, but still close enough to Maxwell Perkins, the editor he relied on to give his work form. "You couldn't find a better place to work," he wrote to the secretary of the Guggenheim Foundation, which had given him a grant to work on his widely anticipated second novel.

In early 1931, Wolfe moved into a ground-floor apartment at 70 Verandah Place near Cobble Hill Park. The rent cost $65 per month. There the massive, boisterous writer worked day and night, fueled by mud-black coffee and cigarettes lit one after the other, all while standing half-naked in front of an open window, using as his desk the door of an old refrigerator. Passersby on

The house at 5 Montague Terrace in Brooklyn Heights, where Thomas Wolfe lived in the 1930s.

the sidewalk across the street often stopped and stared.

Wolfe frequently went on walks at night, through Red Hook and around downtown and over the Brooklyn Bridge, "to escape the suffocation of his apartment and of his own mind," as Evan Hughes writes in his fascinating 2011 book, *Literary Brooklyn*. Sometimes his ambles would take him down to the Gowanus Canal, which Wolfe famously described, eighty years before its designation as a Superfund site, as a "huge symphonic stink," containing traces not only "of a stagnant sewer, but also the smells of melted glue, burned rubber, and smoldering rags… deceased, decaying cats, old tomatoes, rotten cabbage, and prehistoric eggs."

Toward the end of 1931, Wolfe moved to more spacious quarters in nearby Columbia Heights, before finally settling in at 5 Montague

Wolfe minutely described the ingredients comprising the stench of that highly toxic (yet strangely beloved) open sewer known as the Gowanus Canal.

Terrace, in a building that has a plaque commemorating his residency. After the exhaustive, nerve-racking editing process with Perkins led to the nearly thousand-page *Of Time and the River*, Wolfe sat for an interview with the *New York Herald Tribune*. The profile unkindly revealed the slovenliness of his rooms and even listed the actual address. Wolfe saw that it was time to leave. "I have lived here long enough and finished a big job here," he wrote, "and it's time to go." He decamped again for Europe, where he soon got the news he needed: The new novel was a hit.

Three years later, the man many thought the most promising writer of his generation— "the only contemporary writer who can be mentioned in the same breath as Dickens and Dostoevsky," the critic Malcolm Cowley declared—was dead at thirty-seven. *You Can't Go Home Again*, his unfinished novel

about his time in Brooklyn, was published posthumously, in 1940.

WHERE TO VISIT

Thomas Wolfe's longest-lasting apartment in Brooklyn (private)
5 Montague Terrace
Brooklyn, NY 11201

Alfred Kazin was just one of many twentieth-century Brooklyn Jews who made what another, Norman Podhoretz, famously called "one of the longest journeys in the world"—from a Brooklyn ghetto to the heights of literary renown in Manhattan— and became one of the leading literary critics in America. Kazin wrote about his journey in a trilogy of riveting memoirs: *A Walker in the City* (1951), *Starting Out in the Thirties* (1965), and *New York Jew* (1978).

He grew up in a four-bedroom flat in a small brick house at 256 Sutter Avenue. Unlike much else in Brownsville from those bygone times—like the buildings where my own grandparents grew up and the corner luncheonette my great-grandfather ran as a sort of community hall—Kazin's home still stands. Brownsville in the 1920s was 95 percent Jewish, and known as the "Jerusalem of America." Kazin compared it to a Polish or Russian shtetl. Brownsville was the "margin of the city," Kazin recalled, even "the end of the world." All around was "dead land, neither country nor city, with that look of prairie waste I have so often seen on my walks

Ridgewood Reservoir, where Kazin used to go for walks on "still, perfectly hot afternoons."

along the fringes of American cities near the freight yards," he remembered in *Walker*. He often went for walks among the tall trees in Highland Park and around the Ridgewood Reservoir, since decommissioned and filled in by a peaceful meadow.

"Every time I go back to Brownsville," Kazin wrote, "it is as if I had never been away. From the moment I step off the train at Rockaway Avenue and smell the leak out of the men's room, then the pickles from the stand just below the subway steps, an instant rage comes over me, mixed with dread and some unexpected tenderness. It is over ten years since I left to live in 'the city'—everything just out of Brownsville was always 'the city.' Actually I did not go very far; it was enough that I could leave Brownsville. Yet as I walk those familiarly choked streets at dusk and see the old women sitting in front of the tenements, past and present become each other's faces;"—Whitman again!—"I am back where I began."

WHERE TO VISIT

Alfred Kazin's childhood home (private)
256 Sutter Avenue
Brooklyn, NY 11212

In *Brown Girl, Brownstones* (1959), **Paule Marshall**'s semi-autobiographical novel about immigrants from Barbados who live in Brooklyn, the main character, ten-year-old Selina Boyce, is a young girl caught in the middle of her parents' dysfunctional marriage. She is confused about growing up. Her family rents a brownstone in Bedford-Stuyvesant that her mother badly wants to buy; her father, on the other hand, wants to move back to Barbados. The conflict roils the family and ultimately causes it to break apart.

Near the Bed-Stuy brownstone is a green space Selina particularly adores. "Chauncey Street languished in the afternoon heat, and across from it Fulton Park rose in a cool green wall," Marshall writes. "After the house, Selina loved the park. The thick trees, the grass—shrill-green in the sun—the statue of Robert Fulton and the pavilion where the lovers met and murmured at night formed, for her, the perfect boundary for her world; the park was the fitting buffer between Chauncey Street's gentility and Fulton Street's raucousness."

Notable not only for its strong female voice and the perspective of an immigrant class not often depicted in American fiction, *Brown Girl* was well-reviewed on publication, but fell out of print for years until the Feminist Press republished it in the early 1980s. A specific address for the Boyce family's brownstone is not given in the book,

A statue of Robert Fulton, inventor of the steamboat, in the park named after him in Bedford-Stuyvesant.

but in her 2009 memoir *Triangular Road*—named for the connections between Africa, Barbados, and Brooklyn that defined her life—Marshall mentions that she grew up at 501 Hancock Street, just a few blocks from Fulton Park. Bedford-Stuyvesant, Marshall said in an interview, was "the place that had the greatest impression on me."

WHERE TO VISIT

Fulton Park
70 Chauncey Street
Brooklyn, NY 11233

https://www.nycgovparks.org/parks
/fulton-park

Bay Ridge native **Hubert Selby Jr.** is known for two exceptional Brooklyn-based novels. His best-known book, thanks to Darren Aronofsky's 2000 film version, is *Requiem for a Dream* (1978), set largely in Brighton Beach and Coney Island, which concerns the descent of four people into addiction, incarceration, and psychosis.

More evocative of its time and place, however, is *Last Exit to Brooklyn* (1964), set on the South Brooklyn waterfront in present-day Sunset Park and Bay Ridge, around the area of Third Avenue near the Brooklyn Army Terminal. This shocking book contains six connected stories about the seedy side of life in 1950s Brooklyn among the poor underclass left behind by deindustrialization and white (middle-class) flight.

Told in an idiosyncratic, conversational style without conventional punctuation, the book's frank depiction of prostitution, violence, drugs, homosexuality, and cross-dressing made *Last Exit* a scandalous book when it was published by Barney Rosset's Grove Press, an imprint that made something of a specialty of pushing the bounds of decency. Allen Ginsberg, who had faced his own obscenity trial, as Selby did in England, predicted that *Last Exit* would "explode like a rusty hellish bombshell over America and still be eagerly read in a hundred years."

Though it retains a few admirers and champions, the book has fallen somewhat

The Brooklyn Army Terminal, in the once-derelict neighborhood near the waterfront where the interlocked stories of *Last Exit* take place.

out of fashion in recent years, and the gritty dockside neighborhood it depicted has been cleaned up considerably, especially as actual shipping and manufacturing have been replaced on the waterfront by "makerspaces" and expensive condos. But Selby's work is a must-read for a glimpse not only of Brooklyn in its worst days but of the indomitable spirit that prevailed in the borough even then. Despite their flaws, Selby's street-tough characters continue to strive for better. The neighborhood itself becomes the enemy, the embodiment of an uncaring, brutalizing world that beats them down and defeats them, but perhaps not completely.

WHERE TO VISIT

Brooklyn Army Terminal
140 58th Street
Brooklyn, NY 11220
https://www.bklynarmyterminal.com

Jonathan Lethem's fifth novel, *Motherless Brooklyn* (1999), put his native borough back on the literary map. Lionel Essrog, a private investigator with Tourette's syndrome, works for the owner of a local detective agency who is murdered. With his obsessive, detail-fixated mind, Lionel is determined to figure out why.

The book is largely set in the area of Court Street, the commercial strip that heads south from Borough Hall. The street, Lethem writes, is reminiscent of "the old Brooklyn, a placid ageless surface alive underneath with talk, with deals and casual insults, a neighborhood political machine with pizzeria and butchershop bosses and unwritten rules everywhere." It's a world unto itself, vastly different even from Smith Street, just one block away. "Court Street, where it passed through Carroll Gardens and Cobble Hill, was the only Brooklyn, really," Lethem has one of his characters think. The rest of Brooklyn, "everything east of the Gowanus Canal…apart from small outposts of civilization in Park Slope and Windsor Terrace, was an unspeakable barbarian tumult."

Lethem's next book, *The Fortress of Solitude* (2003), followed up with an equally evocative description of Dean Street in the Boerum Hill neighborhood in the late 1970s, on the cusp of gentrification. After years of living on Dean Street, where he was raised, Lethem later decamped for southern California. "Brooklyn is repulsive with novelists, it's cancerous with novelists," Lethem told the *Los Angeles Times*. "That can sometimes be too much."

WHERE TO VISIT

Court Street
Brooklyn, NY 11201

Virginia's Swimming Pony

Misty of Chincoteague, by Marguerite Henry
Chincoteague, Virginia

In 1946, Marguerite Henry traveled to Chincoteague Island, off the coast of mainland Maryland and Virginia. She hoped to see the neighboring Assateague Island's diminutive wild ponies (possibly the descendants of horses that escaped a sinking Spanish galleon) swim across a narrow inlet. The "Pony Penning" event had been going on in one form or another since the seventeenth century, but not until Henry wrote a book based on it did the practice become world-famous.

In the course of her visit, Henry came across a filly named Misty, born in domesticity on the Beebe Ranch, in Chincoteague, with a spot on her side that resembled the rough outline of the continental United States. While in Chincoteague, the author stayed at Miss Molly's Inn on Main Street and began working on a book, largely based on real characters, human and equine, that soon captured children's imaginations all over the world. She purchased Misty from the Beebe family for $150 and had her shipped by train back to Henry's home in Illinois.

Misty of Chincoteague, published in 1947, became an instant best seller, and was named a prestigious Newbery Honor Book for children's literature the following year. The film version, released in 1961, featured many members of the Chincoteague community as extras, though Misty herself didn't appear in it. When the movie premiered, the famous horse, who

The still-active Beebe Ranch, where Henry first saw Misty.

The annual "Pony Penning," in which hundreds of the diminutive quadrupeds swim across a narrow channel to Chincoteague Island.

returned to the Beebe Ranch in 1957, left her hoofprints in the sidewalk outside the town's movie theater. They remain there today.

For devoted *Misty* fans inspired to visit the four-legged icon's favorite spots, the Chincoteague Chamber of Commerce offers a map that guides visitors to "all things Misty" in the town: Travel to the Beebe Ranch for a glimpse of the stall Misty occupied when she lived there, along with photos from her time on the farm. Thanks to the wonders of taxidermy, the horse herself, in all her mischievous glory, is preserved at the Museum of Chincoteague. Stay at Miss Molly's Inn and sleep in the room where Henry began working on the book. And if you visit in late July, you can join tens of thousands of other spectators watching the ponies, including some of Misty's more than two hundred descendants, swim across the channel. When they get to the other side,

the ponies are rounded up and the choicest specimens sold to the highest bidder.

WHERE TO VISIT

Beebe Ranch
3062 Ridge Road
Chincoteague Island, VA 23336

https://www.chincoteaguechamber.com
/directory/beebe-ranch/

Museum of Chincoteague Island
7125 Maddox Boulevard
Chincoteague Island, VA 23336

http://chincoteaguemuseum.com

Miss Molly's Inn
4141 Main Street
Chincoteague Island, VA 23336

https://missmollys-inn.com

The Margaret Mitchell House, where the author lived when she began work on her sweeping novel.

Scarlett O'Hara's Georgia Haunts

Gone with the Wind, by Margaret Mitchell
Atlanta, Georgia

Margaret Mitchell's Civil War epic, *Gone with the Wind*, has been printed thirty million times since its first appearance in 1936.

The author had been fully reconciled, or so she later said, to the possibility that it might only circulate among family and friends. Despite its racist imagery and nostalgia for the Lost Cause, the book is one of the most beloved American novels of all time, and the source, of course, for one of the most beloved American films. More than three-quarters of a century after its publication, literary pilgrims continue to flock to Georgia for a glimpse of the places that inspired Mitchell's book, places inspired by it in turn, and places that tell the story of her life.

A common first stop is the Margaret Mitchell House, a museum in midtown Atlanta. It was in a tiny ground-floor apartment in this redbrick Tudor-revival building that Mitchell and her husband, John Marsh, lived (between 1925 and 1932) while she began working on the novel. Mitchell, known to her friends as Peggy Marsh, hated

Above and above right: Stately Oaks Plantation, in Jonesboro, Georgia, serves as a representation of Scarlett O'Hara's Tara.

the place so much she called it The Dump. These days the museum is filled with period furniture and photographs of the author. Notably, it also has the front door of the set used for scenes at Scarlett's Tara plantation in the 1939 film.

If the front door of the film version of Tara is at the Margaret Mitchell House in Atlanta, where is the rest of the famous set? Frankly, my dear, that's a damn good question. For years it was a mystery. But, as it turns out, the set, flown to Georgia from Hollywood in 1960, was bought by a company that wanted to make it a tourist attraction. The plan foundered, however, and in 1979 a former first lady of the state, Betty Talmadge, bought the set for $5,000. She stored it in a barn at her home near Jonesboro. After her death in 2005, local historian Peter Bonner took on the project of restoring it. He sometimes opens the barn to tours to show off his work.

WHERE TO VISIT

Margaret Mitchell House
979 Crescent Avenue NE
Atlanta, GA 30309

http://www.atlantahistorycenter.com
/explore/destinations
/margaret-mitchell-house

Atlanta Central Library
One Margaret Mitchell Square
Atlanta, GA 30303

http://www.afpls.org/central-library

In Atlanta's Margaret Mitchell Square stands the city's Central Library, a 1980 replacement for the Carnegie-built library that the author's father helped found. This is where Mitchell did research for the book. The library boasts a huge collection of Mitchell memorabilia—some fifteen hundred pieces—including her Remington typewriter, her books, and the Pulitzer Prize she won for the novel.

The Blue Willow Inn
294 North Cherokee Road
Social Circle, GA 30025

https://bluewillowinn.com

Forty-five minutes east of Atlanta, in a town called Social Circle, is the Greek Revival mansion that once belonged to the cousin of Mitchell's first husband, Red Upshaw, the inspiration for Rhett Butler. Now called the Blue Willow Inn, it's a well-known Southern restaurant, famed for its fried chicken and sweet tea. The inn's website brags about visits by former German chancellor Helmut Kohl and generals from the Republic of Georgia. You'll never be hungry again!

Oakland Cemetery
248 Oakland Avenue SE
Atlanta, GA 30312

http://www.oaklandcemetery.com

In 1949, the famous author was walking across Atlanta's Peachtree Street, heading to the movies with her husband, when a speeding Ford driven by an off-duty cabdriver struck her, fracturing her pelvis and skull. Mitchell died of her injuries a few days later. She was buried in the city's iconic Oakland Cemetery, where her tomb is often visited, along with thousands of Confederate graves.

The Gone with the Wind Museum
472 Powder Springs Street SW
Marietta, GA 30064

https://www.gwtwmarietta.com

Marietta, a city thirty minutes northwest of Atlanta, is host to a Gone with the Wind Museum in an old cotton warehouse, dating from 1875, where freight trains thunder past the windows. The cases display artifacts from the film, including the Bengaline gown Scarlett wears on her honeymoon, early movie posters, and an original script that belonged to one of the actors. A small exhibit considers one especially fraught subject from the criticism of the novel: the problematic depiction of the Mammy character, for which Hattie McDaniel became the first black actor to win an Oscar.

Stately Oaks Plantation
100 Carriage Lane
Jonesboro, GA 30236

http://www.atlantastruesouth.com
/gone-with-wind/stately-oaks-plantation/

Mitchell describes Scarlett's plantation from the book, Tara, as five miles outside Jonesboro, in Clayton County. It was based on the country home of her maternal grandmother, which no longer stands, but several plantations have stepped in to serve as replacements. The best one is probably Stately Oaks; the 1839 house includes a sharecropper's cabin, an old schoolhouse, and a country store selling Mitchell paraphernalia. Like many plantation homes in the South, Gone with the Wind's creepily nostalgic take on Confederate history carries over to the tone-deaf promotional materials. "Come and rock a while on the front porch!" the Stately Oaks website beseeches. "Bring back the memories of a simpler time."

The Road to Tara Museum
104 North Main Street
Jonesboro, GA 30236

http://www.atlantastruesouth.com
/gone-with-wind/road-to-tara-museum/

Back in Jonesboro, the old railroad depot is now the Road to Tara Museum. It has lots of memorabilia from the film, including costumes, and a daily bus tour of Civil War sites in the vicinity, along with loads of information about Mitchell, the novel, the film, and local history.

The Mercer Williams House Museum, where the murder at the center of *Midnight* took place.

A Mysterious Murder in Savannah's Old Town

Midnight in the Garden of Good and Evil,
by John Berendt
Savannah, Georgia

The most beautiful and storied house in Savannah, the Southern Lowcountry city full of charming homes, sits at the south-western corner of Monterey Square in the gorgeous historic district. Built in the 1860s, the redbrick Italianate mansion, with tall, arched windows and ironwork balconies, was designed by a leading New York archi-tect for a Confederate general named Hugh W. Mercer—the great-grandfather, as it happens, of songwriting legend Johnny Mercer. Later the building housed the local

Shriners temple before, in the middle of the twentieth century, falling into disrepair. In the late 1960s, Jim Williams, an antiques dealer and devoted preservationist, bought the Mercer House and decided to restore it to its former glory. One of fifty historic properties Williams renovated in the course of his career, the Monterey Square mansion was special: After filling the place with museum-quality antiques and eighteenth-century portraits, Williams made it his home and office.

It was in that house, in May of 1981, sur-rounded by his invaluable collection of royal silverware, Fabergé boxes, and World War II paraphernalia, that Williams shot and killed his young, anger-prone assistant, Danny Hansford—not coincidentally, perhaps, the most notorious gigolo in Savannah. Williams claimed self-defense, alleging that Hansford had tried to shoot him first. Juries that judged the preservationist—ultimately he was tried four separate times for the crime, a state record—seemed to accept that argument. Convicted at first, Williams's verdict was later tossed out. After the final trial, in 1989, Williams threw a lavish party in his own honor. Six months later, he died of pneumonia (possibly related to AIDS), almost in the very spot where he had shot Hansford.

In 1994, the case became the subject of John Berendt's brilliantly atmospheric *Midnight in the Garden of Good and Evil*, an instant best seller and a Pulitzer Prize nominee. With suspenseful pacing and stranger-than-fiction characters, the (closely reported) book reads like a mystery novel. Turned into a movie in 1997, starring Kevin Spacey, Jude Law, and John Cusack, the story of Hansford's murder has helped make the Savannah historic district a tourist-packed destination—with one stop standing out for its literary importance.

Still owned by Jim Williams's sister, but open for public tours, the Mercer House has been kept exactly as it was in his time. The carriage house in the back, where Williams once had his antiques store, is now a gift shop, selling magnets, copies of Berendt's

The Bird Girl, the statue featured on the iconic cover of *Midnight in the Garden of Good and Evil*, was sculpted in 1936 and placed in Bonaventure Cemetery; after the book's publication it was moved to Savannah's Telfair Museum for preservation.

book, and desktop replicas of the eerie statue, which can be seen at the Telfair Museums' Jepson Center for the Arts, that appeared on its iconic cover.

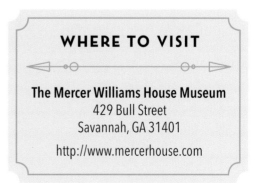

WHERE TO VISIT

The Mercer Williams House Museum
429 Bull Street
Savannah, GA 31401
http://www.mercerhouse.com

The Unsettled Past and Uncertain Future of Atticus Finch's Hometown

To Kill a Mockingbird, by Harper Lee
Monroeville, Alabama

Monroeville, Alabama, has less than seven thousand residents, but more than thirty thousand annual visitors—much more than the number of people who live in the entire Monroe County. Monroeville is the county seat, as is clear from the courthouse in the middle of town—the destination for all those tourists. It's an impressive building, but the people don't come to out-of-the-way Monroeville to take in the architecture. The courthouse, according to a nearby sign, is a "national literary mecca," and Monroeville, north of Mobile and south of Montgomery, the "literary capital of Alabama." Neither is an exaggeration, for Monroeville was the birthplace and lifelong home of Harper Lee, author of the classic *To Kill a Mockingbird.* It's also the novel's setting, thinly disguised as Maycomb, described by Lee as "an island in a patchwork sea of cotton fields and timber land."

Published in 1960, *Mockingbird* has sold more than forty million copies, won a Pulitzer Prize, and spawned an Oscar-winning film. The story centers around a local lawyer named Atticus Finch (father of the narrator, six-year-old Scout) and his defense of Tom Robinson, a black man facing trumped-up charges that he raped a white woman. As Atticus confronts the town's deeply embedded racism, Scout and her friends embark on a campaign to get their reclusive neighbor, Boo Radley, to appear.

Much in the novel, both its characters and setting, is based on real-life people and places that Lee knew from Monroeville. Atticus is modeled after her father, Amasa Coleman Lee, a respected local lawyer who worked at the courthouse. As a child, Lee would watch from the balcony as he argued cases before the judge. In 1919, before she was born, he defended two black men on trial for murder. Unlike Robinson in the book, the men were found guilty and hanged. Lee's father was reportedly so despondent that he gave up criminal law.

The book is set in 1936. The town has been hit badly by the Depression. "Maycomb was an old town, but it was a tired old town when I first knew it," Lee writes in the book, using Scout's voice. "People moved slowly then. They ambled across the square, shuffled in and out of the stores around it, took their time about everything."

The pace in Monroeville is still unhurried, though the town suffers today as it did in the 1930s from a slow economy. Factories have

The Monroe County Courthouse, in Monroeville, Alabama.

been shuttered in recent years and many shops around the courthouse square sit empty. One of its best hopes is its connection to Harper Lee. Before Lee's death in 2016, Monroeville had only one major attraction tied to the novel: the Monroe County Heritage Museum, in the old courthouse. But even there the association was somewhat tenuous: Lee herself once sued the institution to block it from selling *Mockingbird*-

related memorabilia in the gift shop.

Since 1990, Monroeville has played host every April to a performance of a play adapted from the novel, with an all-local cast playing the parts. For years, the town's real sheriff played the sheriff in the drama, and members of the jury are selected from the audience. The first act is performed in an amphitheatre outside the stately building,

The climactic scene of *To Kill a Mockingbird* is performed in the courthouse every year.

and the second in the stately building itself. Over the years, the play has been taken on the road and performed all over the world, from Hong Kong to Chicago to England.

There are a few other places to commune with the book in Monroeville, if one knows where to look and when to go. (The 1962 film was not shot on location, but according to Lee the replica of the courthouse and of the town were incredibly close to reality.) Near the courthouse is the building that used to house the local jail, where in the book

Atticus keeps watch the night before the trial to prevent a mob of drunk, angry whites from lynching Tom. A nearby mural depicts the scene. The jail is now the office of a charity, a far better fate than what has befallen the Lee family's old home: The building is gone and in its place is a fast-food joint.

Lee famously avoided the public spotlight for decades, if not as thoroughly as Boo Radley shuns the outside world—she was private but not reclusive, splitting her time between Monroeville and New York City until 2007, when, after a stroke, she returned to Alabama full time. She shared a home with her beloved sister Alice until the latter's death in 2014, and then entered an assisted-living facility.

Lee became a subject of international attention the following year when her lawyer Tonja Carter announced that she had discovered a first draft of *Mockingbird*, titled *Go Set a Watchman*, and that it would be published—despite Lee's vow never to publish another book. Some suspected that Lee, with her health fading, hadn't given her consent, but authorities investigated and dismissed the claims. When it was published, the book pictured Atticus in a far less heroic light than in *Mockingbird*. Lee's original depiction of Atticus—though it was written first, *Watchman* is set more than twenty years after *Mockingbird*—shows a fairly run-of-the-mill Southern bigot who criticizes Scout's support for the burgeoning civil rights movement.

Harper Lee died in early 2016, and was buried in the family plot at First United Methodist Church in Monroeville. Shortly before the author's death, she formed a new organization called the Mockingbird Company, which quickly moved to take over the annual production of the play. In 2016, after Lee's death, the company fired the director and took other aggressive moves that turned off many of the local actors who had performed in the play—putting the future of the play, and that of the courthouse museum that relied on proceeds from it, in serious doubt.

Under the direction of Carter, the executor of Lee's estate, the Mockingbird Company has bigger plans, too: to dramatically boost the *Mockingbird*-related tourism that comes to town to over 100,000 visitors. Representatives of the company visited Shakespeare's hometown of Stratford-upon-Avon, in England, to come up with business ideas. The current plans are to turn the 1909 building where Lee's father had his law office into a new museum, and to construct replicas of Scout's and Boo Radley's homes. One critic suggested that the plans risked missing the point of the novel in order to drum up feel-good tourism. It would turn Monroeville,

A mural depicts some of the novel's explosive and highly emotional scenes.

one critic told the *Guardian*, into "a Disneyland for racists." Others suggested that the taciturn Lee would have disapproved of the plans, citing a letter she once wrote denouncing the "new holiday sport in Monroeville… That of people bringing their visiting relatives to look at me." That letter itself was sold at auction a year after Lee died.

WHERE TO VISIT

Monroe County Museum at the Old Monroe County Courthouse
31 North Alabama Avenue
Monroeville, AL 36460

https://www.monroecountymuseum.org
/old-courthouse-museum

In Small-Town Arkansas, the Smell of Fear and Guilt

The Memoirs of Maya Angelou
Stamps, Arkansas

Marguerite Johnson—better known as Maya Angelou—was born in St. Louis in 1928. At three years old, following her parents' divorce, the girl and her brother were sent to live with their grandmother in Stamps, Arkansas, a "small, musty town." Segregated and split by railroad tracks, Stamps was dominated by the lumber business. In her spare 1969 memoir, *I Know Why the Caged Bird Sings*, Angelou describes Stamps as a place where she felt both "enormous love, and enormous pain."

The children lived with their grandmother behind the general store she ran— the only black-owned business in town. When her father returned the children to their mother's care in St. Louis, a disastrous time began for Maya; she was molested and then raped by her mother's live-in boyfriend—a horrible exposure to pain and trauma and even guilt, for her assailant was killed not long after the child spoke up. She didn't speak for five years, fearful of the power of her voice.

"In my memory, Stamps is a place of light, shadow, sounds and entrancing odors. The earth smell was pungent, spiced with the odor of cattle manure, the yellowish acid of the ponds and rivers, the deep pots of greens and beans cooking for hours with smoked or cured pork. Flowers added their heavy aroma. And above all, the atmosphere was pressed down with the smell of old fears, and hates, and guilt."

–Maya Angelou,
Gather Together in My Name (1974)

During her years in Arkansas, Angelou attended classes at the segregated Lafayette County Training School, which was listed on the National Register of Historic Places in 2005 as a testament to its role in African-American education.

Returned to Stamps, Maya found refuge in books by Charles Dickens and William Shakespeare and Edgar Allan Poe and James Weldon Johnson. Reading, she later said, gave her back her voice. It was in Stamps, at her eighth-grade graduation, after a white politician blithely insulted the black students, that Angelou sang along with her classmates to Johnson's "Lift Every Voice and Sing," often called the black national anthem. "I was no longer a member of the proud graduating class," she wrote in *Caged Bird*. "I was a member of the proud, graduating, negro race." Also in Stamps is Brown Chapel Christian Methodist Episcopal Church, where the young Angelou got her start as a performer, acting in Easter plays and singing her heart out at church services.

When Angelou died in 2014, flags in Stamps flew at half-mast. City Park was later renamed in her honor. "The truth is you never can leave home," Angelou once told Bill Moyers in a documentary about her childhood. "You take it with you everywhere you go."

WHERE TO VISIT

Brown Chapel Christian Methodist Episcopal Church
516 Oak Grove Road
Stamps, AR 71860

Maya Angelou City Park
Stamps, AR 71860

LITERARY MAP:
NEW ORLEANS

MID-CITY

BIENVILLE STREET

NORTH GALVEZ STREET

CANAL STREET

TULANE AVENUE

SOUTH JEFFERSON DAVIS PARKWAY

SOUTH BROAD AVENUE

SOUTH GALVEZ STREET

TULANE
-GRAVIER

POYDRAS STREET

NORTH RAMPART STREET

CANAL STREET

GERT TOWN

EARHART BOULEVARD

PONTCHARTRAIN EXPRESSWAY

WASHINGTON AVENUE

SOUTH CARROLLTON AVENUE

SOUTH CLAIBORNE AVENUE

EARHART BOULEVARD

CENTRAL
BUSINESS
DISTRICT

POYDRAS STREET

BROADMOOR

MARTIN LUTHER KING JR. BOULEVARD

PONTCHARTRAIN EXPRESSWAY

CLAIBORNE AVENUE

TOLEDANO STREET

SOUTH CLAIBORNE AVENUE

SIMON BOLIVAR AVENUE

FRERET

LASALLE STREET

ANNE RICE

CENTRAL
CITY

ANNE RICE'S
HOUSE

LAFAYETTE CEMETERY

NAPOLEON AVENUE

MILAN

LOUISIANA AVENUE

JEFFERSON AVENUE

THE REILLY

ST. CHARLES AVENUE

LOWER
GARDEN
DISTRICT

GARDEN
DISTRICT

HOME

TOURO

TCHOUPITOULAS STREET

TCHOUPITOULAS STREET

WEST RIVERSIDE

MISSISSIPPI RIVER

4TH S

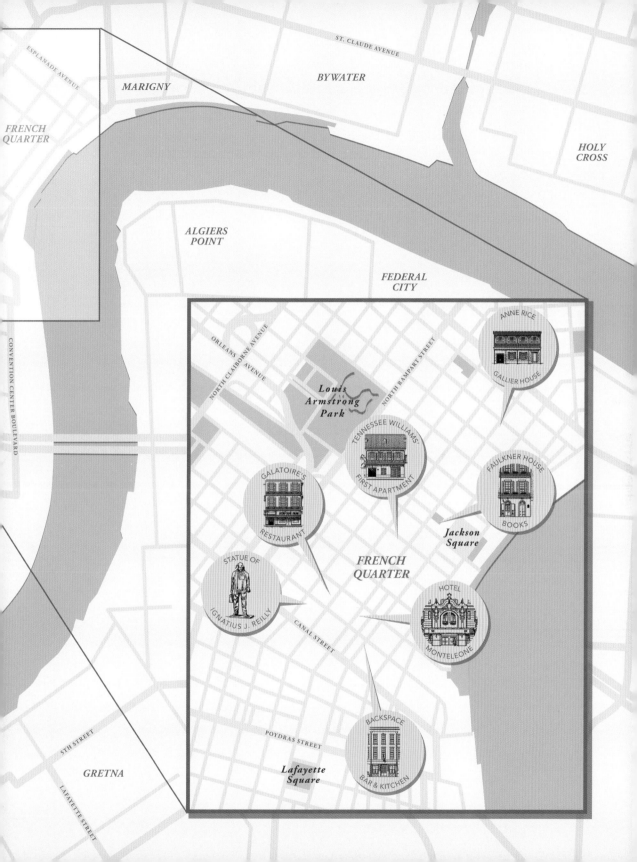

A Spiritual Home in New Orleans

Tennessee Williams, John Kennedy Toole, Anne Rice

To William Faulkner it was "the city where imagination takes precedence over fact." To Tennessee Williams it was the place where creative outcasts were allowed to thrive. "In New York, eccentrics, authentic ones, are ignored," the playwright once wrote. "In Los Angeles, they're arrested. Only in New Orleans are they permitted to develop their eccentricities into art." Over the years, innumerable Crescent City writers have done so, immortalizing its colorful parade of characters, laid-back atmosphere, and multicultural mélange in works of fiction and drama so closely associated with New Orleans it's impossible to imagine them being set anywhere else. Three writers in particular have left their mark on the geography of the Big Easy, placing their favorite haunts and the scenes from their works on the literary map of this spirited city.

Born in Columbus, Mississippi, Thomas Williams grew up in St. Louis. He changed his first name to honor the state his father came from. After trying his luck at different universities, **Tennessee Williams** took a job in a factory and wrote short stories at night, fueled by cigarettes and black coffee. After a nervous breakdown, he traveled all over the country, from New York to southern California, working menial jobs and honing his craft. With a grant from the Rockefeller Foundation, and help from the New Deal's Works Progress Administration, Williams moved to New Orleans to work on his writing full time.

The city, Williams later said, became his "spiritual home." It was where he awakened artistically and sexually, as part of a vibrant art scene in the French Quarter, "the last frontier of Bohemia." He lived in several New Orleans locations at different points in his life. At one place his landlady became so enraged by the late-night partying that she poured scalding water through the floorboards. The police were called and everyone at the gathering had to head to night court. Williams later used the incident for a scene in his 1977 play *Vieux Carré*.

It was while living at another New Orleans residence, on St. Peter Street, that Williams heard "that rattle-trap streetcar named Desire running along Royal and the one called Cemeteries running along Canal," as he wrote in his autobiography, "and it seemed the perfect metaphor for the human condition." The now-famous one ended at Desire Street in the city's Ninth Ward, but the route ceased operation the same year his Pulitzer Prize–winning play appeared on Broadway.

The only home the playwright ever owned in the city was the house at 1014 Dumaine Street, where he lived until his death in 1983. As he wrote in his memoirs, he longed to pass away "in this big beautiful brass bed." The home is not open to the public, but nearby is Lafitte's Guest House, where Williams briefly lived, and 722 Toulouse Street, his first apartment in the city (now part of the Historic New Orleans Collection of buildings), which he called "a poetic evocation of all the cheap rooming houses of the world."

WHERE TO VISIT

**The Historic New Orleans Collection
Louis Adam House**
722 Toulouse Street
New Orleans, LA 70130

https://www.hnoc.org

Galatoire's
209 Bourbon Street
New Orleans, LA 70130

http://www.galatoires.com

The house in the French Quarter where Williams lived as a young writer.

Other stops on a tour of Williams's New Orleans include Galatoire's on Bourbon Street, the writer's favorite restaurant, where he loved to sit at a table near the front window and order Trout Almondine and Shrimp Remoulade. The menu hasn't changed in a century. The Pontchartrain Hotel on St. Charles Avenue proudly displays a page from the *A Streetcar Named Desire* script with hand-scrawled edits on the hotel's 1940s-era stationery. And every spring the city plays host to the Tennessee Williams/New Orleans Literary Festival, drawing more than ten thousand attendees. Don a torn white T-shirt, fall to your knees, clasp your hands to your head: It's not too soon to start practicing for the annual Stella Shouting Competition.

Outside the Hyatt hotel on Canal Street some passersby are surprised to find a statue of a person they can't recognize. He isn't a general or a statesman, neither a well-known author nor a business tycoon. Mustachioed, stocky, wearing a hunting-cap and a flannel shirt, the figure seems to be no kind of hero at all.

That judgment, however, would be a mistake, for the statue depicts one of the unlikeliest heroes in twentieth-century literature: Ignatius J. Reilly, the lethargic, slovenly, flatulent, philosophical lead character in **John Kennedy Toole**'s *A Confederacy of Dunces*.

The statue of Ignatius J. Reilly outside the former Canal Street location of the D. H. Holmes department store.

The statue depicts Reilly in the first scene of the book, as he waits outside the D. H. Holmes department store (founded in 1842, it was open until the early 1990s), while his mother finishes shopping. As he loiters, Reilly busies himself "studying the crowd of people for signs of bad taste in dress."

Born in the Crescent City in 1937, Toole began working on his uproarious novel while serving as an English-language teacher in the US Army in Puerto Rico in the early 1960s. It was a picaresque love letter to the city he missed, full of the Big Easy's oddball characters and motley dialects. For years he tried to interest New York publishers in the novel, but they declined. Toole grew depressed and at one point set off on a cross-country trip; a lifelong admirer of Flannery O'Connor's writing, he tried to visit her house, Andalusia, in Milledgeville, Georgia, but couldn't gain access because it was private. On his way back to New Orleans, Toole stopped in Biloxi, Mississippi, and committed suicide. He was thirty-one years old.

Going through his papers, Toole's mother came across a smudged copy of the manuscript of his unpublished novel, and spent the next decade trying to have it published. She finally got it into the hands of the Southern novelist Walker Percy, then serving as a visiting professor at Loyola University in New Orleans. Percy agreed, albeit reluctantly. While he read, however, Percy slowly realized its promise, as he later wrote in the book's foreword: "First with the sinking feeling that it was not bad enough to quit, then with a prickle of interest, then a growing excitement, and finally an incredulity: surely it was not possible that it was so good." In 1980, Louisiana State University Press finally published the book, and the next year it received the Pulitzer Prize—winning out over one of Percy's own novels.

Other than the statue on Canal Street—put into storage every year to protect it from Mardis Gras revelers—there is one other obvious place to visit in New Orleans related

WHERE TO VISIT

Statue of Ignatius J. Reilly
Hyatt Centric French Quarter New Orleans
800 Iberville Street
New Orleans, LA 70112
https://frenchquarter.centric.hyatt.com
/en/hotel/home.html

The Reilly Home (private)
1032 Constantinople Street
New Orleans, LA 70115

to Toole's unforgettable book. The novel places the Reilly house on Constantinople Street, just off St. Charles Avenue, in an uptown neighborhood that had "degenerated from Victorian to nothing in particular, a block that had moved into the twentieth century carelessly and uncaringly—and with very limited funds." These days that's not a problem: a house claiming to be the Reillys' (dubiously, in the minds of some Toole scholars) sold in 2016 for almost $1 million.

Famous for her richly detailed Vampire Chronicles books, which tell the story of Lestat de Lioncourt, an eighteenth-century French nobleman turned vampire, **Anne Rice** was born in New Orleans, that "strange, decadent city," in 1941. After attending

The nearby Lafayette Cemetery #1 feels appropriately haunted.

school in Texas and San Francisco, where she launched her literary career with *Interview with a Vampire* (1976), Rice returned to New Orleans in 1988 and bought the gorgeous Victorian-Gothic mansion at 1239 First Street in the Garden District, known as the Rosegate House (for its flower-patterned ironwork) and notable for its mammoth columns, tiered porches, and trees covered with moss. In the 1980s, when the goth-fiction craze really took off, hordes of visitors in dark lipstick made pilgrimages to her mansion, often spending several days outside, meeting one another and trying to conjure spirits. Rice encouraged the carnival atmosphere by inviting fans inside and throwing huge Halloween parties.

Not far away is Lafayette Cemetery #1, which includes the Jefferson Fire Company #2 tomb that Rice used as a model for the resting place of the Mayfair witches in *The Witching Hour* (1990). The author once put on a mock funeral in the cemetery to help promote her 1995 novel, *Memnoch the*

Rice's former home in the Garden District.

Devil. Over in the French Quarter is the Gallier House, Rice's model for the bloodsuckers' home in *Interview with the Vampire*, *The Queen of the Damned*, and *The Tale of the Body Thief.*

Every year an official New Orleans fan club puts on a vampire ball. The author herself, who now lives in California, once attended. "I was looking at all of the different people in costume, and I thought, they really know what matters," she told a reporter afterward. "To get out of yourself, to just yield to the imagination."

WHERE TO VISIT

The Rosegate House (private)
1239 First Street
New Orleans, LA 70130

Lafayette Cemetery #1
1416-1498 Washington Avenue
New Orleans, LA 70130

https://www.saveourcemeteries.org
/cemeteries/cemeteries/lafayette-
cemetery-no-1.html

Gallier House
1132 Royal Street
New Orleans, LA 70116

http://www.hgghh.org/about/
gallier-house/

Faulkner House Books.

Other Notable Literary Places in New Orleans

Faulkner House Books, in Pirates Alley, off Jackson Square, is in an 1840 building where William Faulkner lived and wrote (including his first novel, *Soldiers' Pay*) in the bohemian heyday of the 1920s. Known for its excellent collection of first editions, rare volumes, and Southern literature covering every wall from ceiling to floor, this may be the most charming bookstore in the United States.

624 Pirate Alley
New Orleans, LA 70116
https://faulknerhousebooks.com

At the famous **Hotel Monteleone** in the French Quarter, it's not you—the carousel bar is indeed slowly rotating as you sip. (Well, it may also be you, or what you're sipping.) Faulkner, Tennessee Williams, Anne Rice, Eudora Welty, John Grisham, and Ernest Hemingway have all frequented this most famous of New Orleans's many noteworthy establishments for the bookish drinker. Inside the lobby there's a plate-glass display of the books written there, and several suites are named after authors. Truman Capote liked to claim he had been born in the hotel, but his mother, who stayed there during her pregnancy, did in fact make it to the hospital.

The Hotel Monteleone.

214 Royal Street
New Orleans, LA 70130

http://hotelmonteleone.com

139 Chartres Street
New Orleans, LA 70130

http://www.backspacenola.com

To fill up after touring the Big Easy's bookish places, try **Backspace Bar and Kitchen** on Chartres Street, where leather-backed chairs and a roaring fireplace with old volumes lining the mantel offer the right atmosphere for combining, as the website says, literature and libations. Try pairing the roast beef sandwich named for Walt Whitman (who once edited a paper in the city) with a cocktail, Death in the Afternoon (absinthe and champagne), created by Papa Hemingway himself and named for one of his early books.

The Backspace Bar and Kitchen.

Cather's home in Red Cloud.

Home to Red Cloud

The Fiction of Willa Cather
Red Cloud, Nebraska

Born in 1873, in Winchester, Virginia, to a family of Welsh heritage, Willa Cather moved to the tiny village of Red Cloud, Nebraska, when she was nine years old. A difficult period of adjustment followed. "I was little and homesick and lonely," Cather later recalled. "So the country and I had it out together and by the end of the first autumn the shaggy grass country had gripped me with a passion that I have never been able to shake. It has been the happiness and curse of my life."

Cather left home at sixteen to attend college in Lincoln, the state capital, and later spent a decade in Pittsburgh before finally settling in New York. She never returned to live in Red Cloud again. She found it too isolating and stultifying. But, tellingly, she returned to it repeatedly in her fiction. Of the twelve novels Cather published in an extraordinary career—in addition to nearly as many short story collections—six were set in towns based on Red Cloud, though hidden under other names: Moonstone, Haverford, Frankfort, Black Hawk, Sweet Water, and Hanover. It was, however, not so much the town itself as the sprawling prairie surrounding it that inspired Cather's finest writing. Jim Burden, in *My Ántonia*, describes Nebraska's rolling plains as the kind of "place where there was nothing but land: not a country at all, but the material out of which countries were made."

Cather stayed in touch with close friends from Red Cloud and even supported some of them economically through the hard times of the Depression.

When she died in 1947, Cather was buried in New Hampshire, where she spent much of her time later in life.

But it was in Nebraska that she first grasped the essence of life and death, mortality and its opposite. In *My Ántonia*, Cather puts in Jim Burden's mouth her own revelations while lying in the prairie grass. "I kept as still as I could," Burden tells us. "Nothing happened. I did not expect anything to

A stretch of prairie outside town has been preserved and named in her honor.

happen. I was something that lay under the sun and felt it, like the pumpkins, and I did not want to be anything more. I was entirely happy. Perhaps we feel like that when we die and become a part of something entire, whether it is sun and air, or goodness and knowledge. At any rate, that is happiness; to be dissolved into something complete and great. When it comes to one, it comes as naturally as sleep."

The population of Red Cloud is now just over a thousand people, roughly two-thirds of what it was when Cather grew up there, but for such a small town it does an incredibly capable job as a steward of her legacy. In 2017, the twenty-thousand-square-foot National Willa Cather Center opened to the public, complete with a museum (including the author's archive), a research center, apartments for visiting scholars, a bookstore, and a performing arts venue. It's run by the Willa Cather Foundation, a nonprofit founded in 1955 by her first biographer to promote appreciation of her work.

The foundation also preserves a number of buildings in Red Cloud related to Cather and her work, all of which are open to the public for tours—including her childhood home; the house of the young Bohemian-born woman who served as Cather's inspiration for the heroine of *My Ántonia*; the restored 1897 Burlington Depot, featured in many of Cather's works (most notably in the 1905

short story "The Sculptor's Funeral," about the return to town of the body of a dead artist, whose sexuality is called into question); and the 1885 Red Cloud Opera House, now the foundation's headquarters, where Cather gave her high school graduation speech.

For her fans, the most moving place to visit in Red Cloud is the 610-acre Willa Cather Memorial Prairie, preserved just as Cather would have known it, a few miles outside of town. Sitting there beside a pond, among tall grasses, beneath cottonwood trees, it's somehow easy even now, a century and a half after her birth, to think that there's nothing out there but land—that this is not a country at all, but the stuff from which countries are made.

WHERE TO VISIT

National Willa Cather Center
413 North Webster Street
Red Cloud, NE 68970

https://www.willacather.org

Willa Cather Memorial Prairie
Red Cloud, NE 68970

https://www.willacather.org/learn
/cather-prairie

The spooky Clutter house in Holcomb, Kansas.

The Clutter House in Holcomb, Kansas

In Cold Blood, by Truman Capote
Holcomb, Kansas

On the morning of November 16, 1959, the writer Truman Capote was flipping through the *New York Times* when his eye caught a striking headline: "Wealthy Farmer, 3 Of Family Slain." The brief piece reported that a forty-eight-year-old named Herbert W. Clutter and his wife, son, and daughter had been found murdered in their home in the tiny town of Holcomb, Kansas. The authorities had no clue who was responsible; nothing, it seemed, had been taken from the home. "This is apparently the case of a psychopathic killer," the local sheriff told reporters.

Capote, who had made a name for himself a year earlier with the dazzling novella *Breakfast at Tiffany's*, thought about the mysterious murders for a few days before deciding to make them the subject of his next book. He had been thinking for some time about the possibilities of a wholly new literary form—the nonfiction novel—that would combine the imaginative inventiveness of fiction with the real-life characters and situations of journalism. Now he had his subject. "Why not pack up and go to Kansas and see what happens?" Capote later recalled asking himself. "Of course it was a rather frightening thought—to arrive alone in a small, strange town, a town in the grip of an unsolved mass murder. Still, the circumstances of the place being altogether unfamiliar, geographically and atmospherically, made it that much more tempting. Everything would seem freshly minted—the people, their accents and attitudes, the landscape, its contours, the weather. All this, it seemed to me, could only sharpen my eye and quicken my ear."

In the end, he didn't go alone. His friend, the writer Harper Lee, whose Pulitzer Prize–winning *To Kill a Mockingbird* would be published the following year, accompanied him.

The result of six years of research, *In Cold Blood: A True Account of a Multiple Murder and Its Consequences* was a gripping, evocative, groundbreaking work—if something less than the "immaculately factual" account that Capote, who died in 1984, often insisted it was.

The story, in outline, was this: Two criminals, Richard Hickock and Perry Smith, heard from a former cellmate about a wealthy farmer he had once worked for who kept $10,000 hidden in a safe. Hickock and Smith decided to drive hundreds of miles across the state and break into the house to steal the money. When they couldn't find the secret stash—because it didn't exist—they debated what to do. The unstable Smith took the lead. "I didn't want to harm the man," Capote quoted him as later saying. "I thought he was a very nice gentleman. Soft spoken. I thought so right up to the moment I cut his throat."

After that, they killed Clutter's fifteen-year-old son, Kenyon, and sixteen-year-old daughter, Nancy, and his wife, Bonnie—each with a single shotgun blast to the head. They left the house with only a handheld radio, a pair of binoculars, and $50. Six weeks later, following a tip from the former cellmate, police arrested the killers in Las Vegas. Convicted, they were hanged in April 1965.

Capote's book came out nine months after that. Rising to the top of the best-seller lists, it showed publishers that true-crime books could sell big. A 1967 movie version was filmed at the Clutter home, rented out by a new owner, who later sold it to another couple. They became so bothered by the frequent visits from admirers of Capote's book that in the early 1990s they decided to charge $5 for tours of the house. When relatives of the victims complained that they were profiting off a tragedy, the tours were halted. In 2007, the home was put up for sale, but there were no takers—possibly because of the rumor that Nancy Clutter's ghost continues to haunt the premises. A visitor at an open house snapped a picture of some kind of faded red substance on a basement wall—perhaps, some morbidly speculated, traces of Herbert Clutter's blood.

The Clutter house, made famous by Capote, is the best-known tourist attraction for miles around. Be aware, however, that it's still in private hands: Signs at the foot of the driveway warn trespassers to stay away.

WHERE TO VISIT

The Clutter House (private)
Oak Street
Holcomb, KS 67851

What Was Ideal, What Was Base

The Bluest Eye, by Toni Morrison
Lorain, Ohio

When *New Yorker* writer Hilton Als visited 2245 Elyria Avenue, in Lorain, Ohio, in 2003, he found a bright-green two-story house—abandoned, its porch covered in belongings from previous tenants and most of the windows boarded up. The industrial city along Lake Erie, west of Cleveland, had seen better days: specifically, the 1930s and 1940s, when Chloe Wofford—Toni Morrison—was first learning the ways of the world. "Ohio," the author later observed, "is a curious juxtaposition of what was ideal in this country and what was base."

The child of a welder and a devout church singer, the young Morrison knew there were racial tensions in the town, but it wasn't as bad as in the South her parents had fled. Indeed, the celebrated author once told NPR host Terry Gross that she "didn't really have a strong awareness of segregation and the separation of races until I left Lorain."

Not far from the Elyria Avenue house is the building on Broadway that Morrison used as the inspiration for the Breedlove family's home in her first novel, *The Bluest Eye.* Published in 1970, while Morrison was a book editor at Random House, the novel tells the story of a young black girl who wishes she had light skin and blue eyes; horrifically, she is raped and impregnated by her own father. "Visitors who drive to this tiny town wonder why it has not been torn down," Morrison wrote of the house in the book, "while pedestrians, who are residents of the neighborhood, simply look away when they pass it."

In 1993, Morrison became the first African-American to win the Nobel Prize in Literature. Two years later, the Lorain Public Library opened a reading room named in her honor.

WHERE TO VISIT

Lorain Public Library
351 West 6th Street
Lorain, OH 44052
http://www.lorainpubliclibrary.org

The Tortured Relationship of a Minnesota Town and Its Native Son

Main Street, by Sinclair Lewis
Sauk Centre, Minnesota

Sinclair Lewis was born on South Third Street in Sauk Centre, Minnesota, in 1885, the third son of the local doctor and a mother who tragically died when he was just six years old. By then the family had moved across the street to the house where he would grow up and first begin to write. As a thirteen-year-old, Lewis tried to run away and join the troops heading to Cuba to fight in the Spanish-American War. Brought back home, he took a job at the newly built Palmer House Hotel, the first building in town with electricity. It was only four blocks from his home, at the corner of Main Street.

Lewis finally left Sauk Centre at the age of seventeen to attend Oberlin College, before moving on to Yale. It was there, as an undergraduate, that Lewis published his first short story. He moved around, working for different newspapers and publishing a few novels, mostly potboiler fiction and works for hire. (One gig had him selling story lines for novels to the famous Jack London.) After moving to Washington, DC, in 1916, Lewis began working on a realistic novel loosely based on his hometown: the people, the places, and, more than anything else, the stultifying atmosphere.

The book was a breakthrough for Lewis and the first literary smash hit of the century. Set in the small Minnesota town of Gopher Prairie, an obvious stand-in for Sauk Centre, *Main Street: The Story of Carol Kennicott* (1920) presented a scathing critique of the small-mindedness and hidebound conservatism of mainstream American life. The assertive, even proto-feminist title character,

Sinclair Lewis's boyhood home.

reportedly based on the author's formidable stepmother, moves to her husband's new town with a sense of excitement. She expects it will be quaint and charming; she will be sorely disappointed. She dreams of fleeing, but by the end of the book has become more or less reconciled to the place. "Her active hatred of Gopher Prairie had run out," Lewis writes. "She saw it now as a toiling new settlement."

Like many critical portrayals of a place, *Main Street* angered locals who recognized themselves and their neighbors in its pages. They felt betrayed—some residents never forgave Lewis for the treachery.

In the rest of the county, however, the book was a huge hit, selling millions of copies in the first two years. Lewis was rich. He followed that success with other major novels like *Babbitt* (1922), a critique of crass commercialism; *Arrowsmith* (1925), which told the story of a progressive-minded doctor; and *Elmer Gantry* (1927), about a hypocritical minister—all of which had large sections set in a small midwestern city, Zenith (possibly based on Cincinnati), in the fictional state of Winnemac.

In 1930, Lewis became the first American writer to win the Nobel Prize. He delivered a blistering speech about "The American Fear of Literature," in which he

Main Street in Sauk Centre, the hometown Lewis satirized in his most famous work.

explained to his Swedish audience why his native country had not (yet) produced many top-flight writers. "In America most of us—not readers alone, but even writers—are still afraid of any literature which is not a glorification of everything American, a glorification of our faults as well as our virtues," Lewis observed. That was too bad because the country offered a multitude of subjects fit for fiction; it was, he remarked, "the most contradictory, the most depressing, the most stirring, of any land in the world today." Almost a century later that is hardly less true.

Eleven novels came after the Nobel, few

of which were considered equal to the earlier work. One of them, however, has recently earned a new lease on life. *It Can't Happen Here*, his 1935 novel about the rise of a fascist president, became a top-ten best seller on Amazon in the weeks after the 2016 presidential election.

After World War II, in which his eldest son lost his life, Lewis briefly returned to Minnesota and lived in Duluth. Suffering from loneliness and a weakness for drink, the writer died in Rome in 1951. After his body was cremated, the ashes were buried, on his request, in Sauk Centre's Greenwood Cemetery, marked by a gravestone simply describing the deceased as the AUTHOR OF MAIN STREET.

One hundred miles northwest of Minneapolis, Sauk Centre's population is now triple what it was in Lewis's day; it's also at least marginally more diverse, with a modest Hispanic population and a fairly thriving downtown. It's still a small town, dominated by agriculture and a little manufacturing. Though there's a Sinclair Lewis Park and a Gopher Prairie Motel, and local sports teams call themselves the Mainstreeters, Sauk Centre's relationship to its most famous resident remains fraught.

In the 1950s, Lewis's boyhood home was bought by the Sinclair Lewis Foundation and restored to its condition during the author's time. Now its rooms are filled with belongings of the Lewis family, including the tiny bed he slept in as a child, and the house is open for tours. The foundation also hosts an annual writers' conference in Lewis's honor. The street the house is on has been renamed Sinclair Lewis Avenue.

In 1975, with Senator Hubert Humphrey cutting the ribbon, Sauk Centre dedicated a Sinclair Lewis Interpretive Center, near Interstate 94, to tell the story of his life and celebrate his work. As the years passed, however, and Lewis's work continued to fall further out of the American canon, the museum lapsed into a state of neglect. In 2016, after a years-long battle, the town closed the interpretive center and put the property up for sale—presumably to some kind of chain-store retailer. The Sauk Centre town planner responsible for the move admitted to a reporter that she had never read Lewis's work. "Babbitt won out," a member of the foundation's board told the *Minneapolis Star-Tribune*. As of this writing, the property has not yet been sold.

The people of Sauk Centre seem not yet to have entirely forgiven, much less embraced, the Nobel Prize–winning author who shined a harsh light on the limitations of their lives. For his part, Lewis thought people took his criticisms of small-town American life too hard. "I am quite certain," he once said, "that I could have been born and reared in no place in the world where I would have had more friendliness. It was a good time, a good place, and a good preparation for life."

WHERE TO VISIT

Sinclair Lewis Boyhood Home
810 Sinclair Lewis Avenue
Sauk Centre, MN 56378
http://www.sinclairlewisfoundation.com
/boyhood_home/boyhood_home.htm

A Magic Bus in the Alaskan Woods

Into the Wild, by Jon Krakauer
Healy, Alaska

On April 28, 1992, a twenty-four-year-old California native walked into the wilderness west of Healy, Alaska, with ten pounds of rice, a rifle, four hundred rounds of ammunition, a camera, and some books. The driver of a pickup who dropped off the strange hitchhiker at the trailhead was so concerned about the man's lack of provisions that he made him take a pair of boots. He was right to be concerned: 131 days later, a backcountry hunter found the emaciated body of Christopher McCandless decomposing inside a sleeping bag in an abandoned bus. He weighed just sixty-six pounds.

The story of Christopher McCandless's searching life and lonely death was first told by the journalist Jon Krakauer in a 1993 story for *Outside* magazine, later turned into a best-selling 1996 book, *Into the Wild*, now a classic of late twentieth-century American nonfiction. The 2007 film version, directed

The bus where Chris McCandless died remains right where it was when he found it—though in considerably worse shape.

and produced by Sean Penn, brought to a new audience the tale of a young man, influenced by the writings of Henry David Thoreau and Jack London, who grew tired of mainstream society and sought a truer, purer relationship to nature and to himself by seeking solitude in the Alaska woods.

Well, that, or he was a narcissistic ignoramus with a nasty case of the death wish—it depends who you ask.

Apparently, McCandless's original plan had been—incredibly—to walk all the way to the Bering Sea. But when the thick-grown Alaskan bush proved too formidable an obstacle, McCandless turned back to set up camp at a broken-down bus he had seen

along the Stampede Trail a few miles back. It was a green-and-white 1946 International Harvester, originally built for the Fairbanks public transit system and last used in the early 1960s as temporary shelter by workers building a road to a mine on the edge of nearby Denali National Park. The workers abandoned it near the banks of a river because it had a broken axle.

In his months at the bus, McCandless foraged for plants and berries and hunted geese, porcupine, and, on one triumphant occasion, a moose. By July, however, he had had enough, and tried to hike back to civilization. He found his route blocked, however, by the same river he had first crossed in early spring; now it had swollen with snowmelt and was impassible. He hadn't taken any maps on the great adventure, so he didn't know that a hand-cranked tram across the river was less than a mile away.

Despite still-continuing rounds of investigations and revised analyses by Krakauer and others, it's not quite clear what killed McCandless. In a journal entry near the end, he seemed to blame toxic potato seeds he had inadvertently consumed. He grew too weak to get out of bed, and couldn't hunt to stay alive. "MUCH TROUBLE JUST TO STAND UP," he wrote in late July. "STARVING. GREAT JEOPARDY."

The bus is still there. An Alaskan journalist who snowmobiled to the site in 2003

The Alaskan wilderness, outside the town of Healy.

described the wreck as "the most absurd thing you could imagine encountering in this open, white space." Known as the "Magic Bus," it's a popular destination for literary pilgrims seeking the meaning of life, communion with McCandless's spirit, or a shareable picture—like the one found on the departed pilgrim's camera after his death—of themselves leaning back on a folding chair against the bus. Inside, near the bed McCandless died in, a plaque installed by his family commemorates his "adventurous travels in search of how he could best realize God's great gift of life." When they visited in 1993, McCandless's parents also left a store of emergency supplies to save anyone else from succumbing to his fate, as well as notebooks now filled with comments left by the hundreds of visitors who have followed in his footsteps.

Over the years, pilgrims have etched their homespun wisdom into the rusting metal walls and roof. "Stop Trying to Fool Others as the Truth Lies Within," one sage advises. "Live the Life You Always Imagined," suggests another, adapting a quote from Thoreau. Another philanthropist has left a more practical message for the site's apparently careless visitors: "Keep This Place Clean You Human Pigs." Sadly, the increased traffic in recent years has taken its toll, visible in the form of bullet holes, litter, and a general state of deterioration.

Anyone planning to visit the bus should know that it's a long and difficult three-day round-trip along the Stampede Trail and across two fast-moving rivers. Be sure to have all the necessary information and equipment to make the trek in and out, and don't be ashamed to back out if the going gets rough. Every year, several hikers have to be rescued from the trail. In 2010, a visitor from Switzerland drowned while trying to cross the river that kept McCandless hemmed in. And, above all, don't go alone. As McCandless wrote in his notebook: "Happiness only real when shared." That revelation came to him all too late.

For an easier and far less dangerous option, visit the replica bus that was used for filming the 2007 movie version. It's on the grounds of 49th State Brewing Company in the nearby town of Healy, ten miles from the entrance to Denali National Park. The brewery's website makes a pretty good case:

"You can still walk 20 miles through mosquito-infested tundra and risk your life crossing the Teklanika River to get a photo next to the 'Magic Bus'"—or you can visit the replica and walk twenty yards to consider the deep questions of self, solitude, and society over a juicy burger and a hand-crafted beer.

WHERE TO VISIT

Denali National Park and Preserve
Alaska 99755

https://www.nps.gov/dena/index.htm

49th State Brewing Company
Mile 248.4 Parks Highway
Healy, AK 99743

https://www.49statebrewing.com/denali/

The Vampiric Pleasures of Forks, Washington

The Twilight Trilogy by Stephenie Meyer
Forks, Washington

"In the state of Washington, under a near constant cover of clouds and rain, there's a small town named Forks. Population, 3,120 people. This is where I'm moving."

So the seventeen-year-old Bella Swan, teenage heroine, tells us at the beginning of Stephenie Meyer's young-adult blockbuster, *Twilight*, published in 2005. She's leaving Phoenix, where she has lived with her "erratic, hare-brained mother," who is hitting the road with her new husband. Bella

The vampires in the Twilight trilogy like the deep, sunless woods of Olympic National Forest.

isn't thrilled, but she's willing to try out a new place.

Once in Forks, Bella falls in love with Edward Cullen. Unfortunately for her (or so one would think), dear Edward and his entire family turn out to be vampires. Frightened at first (understandably), Bella becomes intrigued.

Strangely, Meyer never visited Forks before she wrote the book. She just figured that with 120 inches of rainfall every year it was probably just the kind of dark and gloomy spot that a family of all-American vampires *would* live in. She even wanted to name the novel after the town until her publisher insisted on changing it.

Tucked in the foothills of the Olympic Mountains, across Puget Sound from Seattle, Forks's economy used to be based on logging. Now it's based on vampires. Catapulted to international fame by the 2008 film version of *Twilight*, starring Kristen Stewart and Robert Pattinson, the town has made the most of its connection to the billion-dollar franchise. The local Chamber of Commerce offers a map of all the book-related locations around town, and also runs the local visitors center, where Bella's famous red Chevy truck from the 1950s is on display, with cutouts of the main characters in the front seat. The Miller Tree Inn, a bed-and-breakfast that calls itself the home of the Cullen house, offers rooms themed for each character from the book, while a local family that owns one of the few two-story houses around town has kindly volunteered it as the Swan family residence, marked by a photo-friendly sign out front.

For other *Twilight* destinations in town, there's Forks High School, where Bella first spots Edward in the cafeteria and finds

In Forks, the Chamber of Commerce has purchased two red trucks to serve as stand-ins for Bella Swan's.

there's something a little off about him, and the Forks Hospital, which actually reserves a "vampires only" parking spot for Dr. Cullen, the fictional member of its staff. Every September, the town hosts a "Forever Twilight" festival to celebrate Bella's birthday.

In nearby Port Angeles, there's Bella Italia, the aptly named restaurant where the unhappy couple goes on their first date; Bella's order, the mushroom ravioli, can be ordered over the internet. Outside town there's the Olympic National Forest, setting for the woodsy scenes, such as when Edward discloses his secret blood-drinking proclivities. According to the rangers, some *Twilight* fans like to go on hikes through the forest dressed as their favorite characters.

WHERE TO VISIT

Forks Chamber of Commerce
1411 South Forks Avenue
Forks, WA 98331
http://forkswa.com

The Miller Tree Inn
654 East Division Street
Forks, WA 98331
http://millertreeinn.com

Bella Italia
118 East First Street
Port Angeles, WA 98362
http://bellaitaliapa.com

Nirvana at Desolation Peak

The Dharma Bums, by Jack Kerouac
North Cascades, Washington

"What a name, Desolation, oo, wow, ugh, wait…"

Two-thirds of the way into his fourth novel, *The Dharma Bums*, Jack Kerouac's stand-in narrator is listening to his friend, a Buddhist mountaineer named Japhy Ryder (based on the poet Gary Snyder), explain what an enlightenment-seeker can expect from a season at a fire-tower lookout in the North Cascade Mountains. At Snyder's suggestion, Kerouac has decided to spend the next summer alone atop a peak on the rugged border between Washington State and British Columbia. He is looking for salvation, not desolation, and the name of the mountain on which he will serve his time has him a little concerned. He need not be, for one of the things he will learn is that emptiness and awakening are very often the same thing.

It was the summer of 1956 and thirty-four-year-old Kerouac was still searching for truth. After a decade of boozy poetry readings and endless traipsing back and forth across America, he was turning his attention to the power of nature to cleanse and heal the human soul. He had already written what would become his masterpiece, *On the Road*, but hadn't yet found a publisher. "I came to a point where I needed solitude and [to] just stop the machine of 'thinking' and 'enjoying' what they call 'living,'" he later recalled. "I just wanted to lie in the grass and look at the clouds."

How better to do that than by spending two months in a white-framed cabin 6,600 feet above sea level and fifteen miles from the nearest road? "On Desolation," Kerouac wrote, "I was the alonest man in the world."

His journey there was an odyssey in itself. From Snyder's cabin in the woods north of San Francisco, Kerouac hitchhiked up to the Olympic peninsula and took a fifty-cent ferry across Puget Sound. For the first time he took in the "miles and miles of unbelievable mountains grooking on all horizons in the wild broken clouds." In Seattle—"wet, immense, timbered, mountainous, cold, exhilarating, challenging"—he washed up at a hotel and the next morning caught a ride

The cabin where Kerouac went to "stop the machine of 'thinking.'"

Hozomeen, the mountain Kerouac became fixated on during his time in the lookout tower.

toward the Cascades, those "unbelievable jags and twisted rock and snow-covered immensities, enough to make you gulp."

The road ran right through the dreamy fertile valleys of the Stilaquamish and the Skagit, rich butterfat valleys with farms and cows browsing under that tremendous background of snow-pure heaps. The further north I hitched the bigger the mountains got till I finally began to feel afraid.

A few more days of hiking, boating, riding an old incline railway, boating again, and horseback riding—while receiving some basic fire-watching training along the way—brought Kerouac, with a summer's worth of provisions, to the top of Desolation Peak. His only contact with the outside world would be a small two-way radio. Years later, a former colleague in the Forest Service complained that Kerouac sometimes turned the radio off to focus on his writing.

He did not, in fact, get much writing done—but some of the most evocative pages

Kerouac wrote after *On the Road* were about his time on Desolation Peak. In *Lonesome Traveller*, a 1960 collection of sketches and journal entries, Kerouac described the view from his "alpine yard" on his first morning atop the mountain:

> …hundreds of miles of pure snow-covered rocks and virgin lakes and high timber…a sea of marshmallow clouds flat as a roof and extending miles and miles in every direction…on my 6600-foot pinnacle it was all far below me… And it was all mine, not another human pair of eyes in the world were looking at this immense cycloramic universe of matter. I had a tremendous sensation of its dreamlikeness which never left me all that summer and in fact grew and grew, especially when I stood on my head to circulate my blood, right on top of the mountain…

In the evening he took in the "mad raging sunsets pouring in sea foams of cloud through unimaginable crags like the crags you grayly drew in pencil as a child, with every rose-tint of hope beyond."

Kerouac became obsessed with the twin-peaked giant of Hozomeen, a nearby mountain two thousand feet higher than Desolation. "Hozomeen, Hozomeen, the most mournful mountain I ever seen…" he sings in *The Dharma Bums*. He comes to think of its "stark naked rocks" as "the Void."

As his time on the mountain came to an end—and none too soon—Kerouac resolved not to forget what he had learned on the mountain: that total isolation from the world was not necessary for pulling back the veil and perceiving its hidden realities. "I decided that when I would go back to the world down there I'd try to keep my mind clear in the midst of murky human ideas smoking like factories on the horizon through which I could walk, forward…"

These days, Desolation Peak remains a favored destination for literary pilgrims with dog-eared paperbacks stuffed in rucksacks. Instagrammers among them often do head-stands in front of Hozomeen. It takes some logistical planning to get to the trailhead: either a boat across Ross Lake or a long hike in from Highway 20. Permits can be secured for overnight camping a mile down from the peak or along the shoreline of the lake. Bring water.

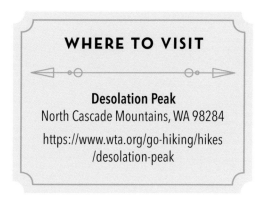

WHERE TO VISIT

Desolation Peak
North Cascade Mountains, WA 98284
https://www.wta.org/go-hiking/hikes
/desolation-peak

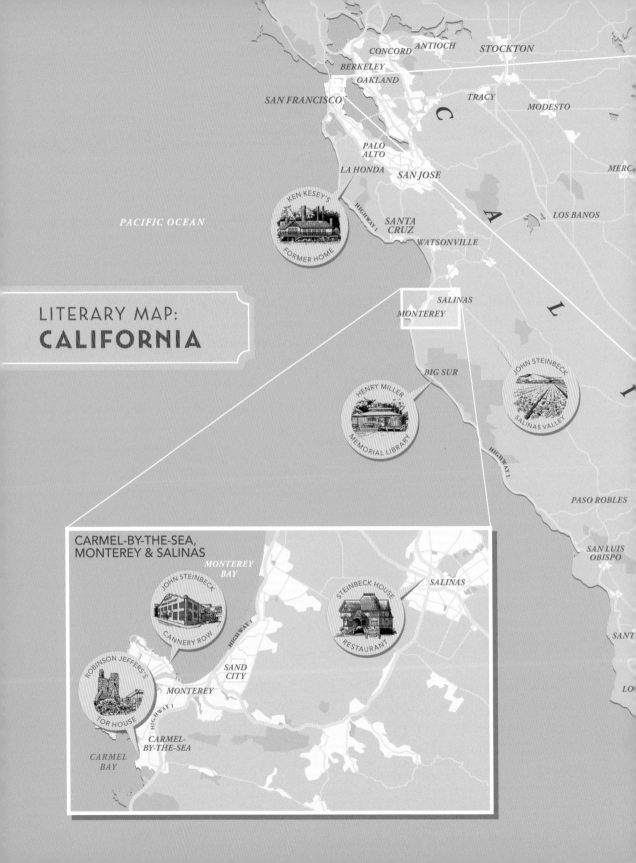

LITERARY MAP: CALIFORNIA

PACIFIC OCEAN

CONCORD ANTIOCH STOCKTON
BERKELEY
OAKLAND
SAN FRANCISCO
TRACY
MODESTO

PALO
ALTO
LA HONDA
SAN JOSE
MERC.

SANTA
CRUZ
WATSONVILLE
LOS BANOS

KEN KESEY'S FORMER HOME

HIGHWAY 1

C

A

L

I

SALINAS
MONTEREY

BIG SUR

HENRY MILLER MEMORIAL LIBRARY

JOHN STEINBECK SALINAS VALLEY

HIGHWAY 1

PASO ROBLES

SAN LUIS
OBISPO

SANT

LO

CARMEL-BY-THE-SEA, MONTEREY & SALINAS

MONTEREY
BAY

JOHN STEINBECK CANNERY ROW

HIGHWAY 1

SAND
CITY

SALINAS

STEINBECK HOUSE RESTAURANT

ROBINSON JEFFERS'S TOR HOUSE

MONTEREY

HIGHWAY 1

CARMEL-
BY-THE-SEA

CARMEL
BAY

NORTH BEACH, SAN FRANCISCO

Yosemite National Park

SAN FRANCISCO BAY

Fort Mason

BAY STREET

NORTH BEACH

COLUMBUS AVENUE

THE BEAT MUSEUM

LOMBARD STREET

RUSSIAN HILL

VAN NESS AVENUE

BROADWAY

CITY LIGHTS BOOKSELLERS

VESUVIO CAFÉ

THE EMBARCADERO

CHINATOWN

Lafayette Park

NOB HILL

FINANCIAL DISTRICT

PINE STREET

BUSH STREET

MARKET STREET

MISSION STREET

1ST STREET

DWIGHT D. EISENHOWER HIGHWAY

Sequoia National Forest

RIDGECREST

F

O

BAKERSFIELD

R

N

BARSTOW

I

Los Padres National Forest

LANCASTER

PALMDALE

RAYMOND CHANDLER

VICTORVILLE

A

SANTA BARBARA

GREYSTONE MANSION

HESPERIA

HIGHWAY 1

Angeles National Forest

OXNARD

THOUSAND OAKS

BURBANK

SAN BERNARDINO

SANTA MONICA

BEVERLY HILLS

PASADENA

HIGHWAY 1

LOS ANGELES

RIVERSIDE

ANAHEIM

City Lights Booksellers & Publishers in the North Beach section of San Francisco has been run by poet Lawrence Ferlinghetti since he cofounded it in 1953.

A Literary Road Trip Down the California Coast

The Beats, the Hippies, John Steinbeck, Robinson Jeffers, Henry Miller, Raymond Chandler

Few places in the world have been the subject of as much important (and inspiring) literature as the California coast, the place, as Jack Kerouac writes in *On the Road*, that marks "the end of America—no more land." To drive down the famous Highway 1 from San Francisco to Los Angeles is to travel through territories defined by their treatment in fiction, memoir, and poetry by some of the greatest American writers, from the soul-searching travelogues of the San Francisco Beats to the hard-boiled detective novels of Raymond Chandler, Dante of the Los Angeles night. While not nearly exhaustive of the many Golden State locations that have been featured in fiction, these stops would make for a fine north-to-south road trip, a good sample of all the enchanted coast—and California-based literature—has to offer.

Literary pilgrims have been descending on the North Beach section of San Francisco since the 1950s, when the **Beat writers—**

especially Allen Ginsberg, Jack Kerouac, and William S. Burroughs—first raised the flag of postwar American countercultural revolt. San Francisco, its "eleven mystic hills with the blue Pacific and its advancing wall of potato-patch fog beyond, and smoke and goldenness in the late afternoon of time," as Kerouac wrote in *On the Road*, was the movement's mecca; City Lights bookstore on Columbus Avenue their *kaaba*. The first paperback-only bookstore in the country when it opened in 1953, it's still owned by cofounder Lawrence Ferlinghetti, nearly one hundred years old (as of this writing). In 1955, the bookstore's (still-extant) poetry imprint put out one thousand copies of Ginsberg's *Howl* and triggered a major obscenity trial in which a judge ultimately ruled the poem of "redeeming social importance," and fit for publication.

These days City Lights maintains its cultural vibrancy and countercultural ethos even in a city increasingly dominated by start-up capital. (ABANDON ALL DESPAIR, YE WHO ENTER HERE, a sign over the entrance reads.) It plays host to poetry readings several times every week.

Next door is the pedestrian-only Jack Kerouac Alley, with its massive, colorful murals showing his travels through Mexico and quotes from Kerouac and John Steinbeck. Also next to the alley is Vesuvio Café, the bar where several Beat writers (and Dylan Thomas

and Bob Dylan) wrote and hung out. Just across the street is the relatively new Beat Museum, which has a still-growing collection, including personal effects, like Allen Ginsberg's typewriter and Jack Kerouac's tweed jacket, and various pieces of memorabilia, such as letters, manuscripts, and first editions. The museum also hosts readings and offers walking tours of Beat-related haunts throughout the North Beach neighborhood.

WHERE TO VISIT

City Lights Booksellers & Publishers
261 Columbus Avenue
San Francisco, CA 94133

http://www.citylights.com

The Beat Museum
540 Broadway
San Francisco, CA 94133

http://www.kerouac.com

Vesuvio Café
255 Columbus Avenue
San Francisco, CA 94133

http://www.vesuvio.com

On the night of Saturday, August 7, 1965, Ken Kesey, author of *One Flew Over the Cuckoo's Nest* (1962), threw a notorious party at his ranch in La Honda, California, forty miles south of San Francisco. Kesey—who had first tried LSD as a subject in Project MKUltra, the CIA's experimental mind-control program—was by then the leader of the Merry Pranksters, a motley crew of dropouts. Still three months away was the first of the Pranksters' official Acid Tests, the series of wild LSD-fueled parties soundtracked by a hot new band called the Warlocks (soon renamed the Grateful Dead).

Apple Jack's tavern in La Honda, just down the road from Ken Kesey's place and a famous biker bar in its own right.

This party had a special purpose. THE MERRY PRANKSTERS WELCOME THE HELL'S ANGELS read a fifteen-foot red, white, and blue banner spanning the entrance to Kesey's ranch.

What happened next—one of the formative moments of the 1960s counterculture—has been described in at least three important works: *Hell's Angels*, the first book by gonzo journalist Hunter S. Thompson; *The Electric Kool-Aid Acid Test*, Tom Wolfe's whoop-dang FREAKISH!!! account of the Pranksters' treks across the country in a school bus named Furthur; and in a poem by Allen Ginsberg—"First Party at Ken Kesey's with Hell's Angels"—which mentions the police cars parked outside the gate, their "red lights revolving in the leaves." Both books, but not Ginsberg's poem, describe in graphic detail the gang rape of a young woman at the party, passages that fifty years later are difficult to read.

Kesey sold the property in 1997 to pay off debts from a lawsuit brought by a police officer who fell off the entrance bridge and into La Honda Creek while busting up a party a few years earlier. The yellow, two-bedroom cabin, surrounded by redwoods, lay unoccupied for several years but more recently has been remodeled. It's a mile west on La Honda Road from Apple Jack's Inn, the notorious local biker bar. Bordering the property is the 5,759-acre La Honda Creek Open Space Preserve.

WHERE TO VISIT

Ken Kesey's former home (private)
7940 La Honda Road
La Honda, CA 94020

La Honda Creek Open Space Preserve
Redwood City, CA 94062
https://www.openspace.org/preserves
/la-honda-creek

When the National Steinbeck Center opened on Main Street in Salinas in 1998, built at a cost of $11 million, it was the largest museum in the world devoted to a single author. The expense shows: The lavishly produced exhibits walk visitors through the story of **John Steinbeck**'s life as seen in his work—dozens of novels and short story collections—and includes one really cool artifact in particular: Rocinante, the modified GMC pickup truck he drove around the country in 1960 with a highly personable French poodle. Two years later, after his travelogue of the trip, *Travels with Charley*, was published, Steinbeck was awarded the Nobel Prize in Literature.

Steinbeck was born in Salinas in 1902 and spent his childhood exploring the nooks and crannies of the Salinas Valley. How he felt about the area is perhaps best summed up in the title of his first short story collection: *The*

Monterey's economy, while still largely centered on agriculture, has also been infused by literary tourists who flock to Cannery Row.

The Salinas Valley of California was made famous in the work of John Steinbeck.

Pastures of Heaven. Yet, like many writers, the author had a somewhat uneasy relationship with his hometown. Families who recognized themselves in *East of Eden* (1952) wanted his books banned from the local libraries. When *The Grapes of Wrath* came out in 1939, some townspeople who objected to the book's left-wing politics burned copies of it right on Main Street. Years later, Steinbeck added to the acrimony by writing that "Salinas was never a pretty town…and we knew it."

Still, he made sure he was laid to rest after his death in 1968 in the Garden of Memories, the family cemetery on the edge of town. "No man should be buried in alien soil," he said near the end of his life.

These days, it's no exaggeration to say that the struggling city of Salinas—with a population around 150,000—draws what little vitality it has from its connection to its famous native son. (The Steinbeck museum was an attempt, neither a complete success nor an utter failure, to redevelop the downtown area.) The home he was raised in has been turned into a restaurant that serves lunch in the family's dining room and raises money to keep the house open. He wrote early works like *The Red Pony* (1933) and *Tortilla Flat* (1935) in a bedroom upstairs. East of town is the Gabilan Range, capped by Fremont Peak, described in the opening pages of *East of Eden* as the best place to see the region, from the farmland of the Salinas Valley to the rocky shores of Monterey. "This solitary stone peak overlooks the whole of my childhood and youth," Steinbeck wrote in *Travels with Charley*, describing his final visit to the place of his birth, "the great Salinas Valley stretching south nearly a hundred miles, the town of Salinas where I was born spreading like crabgrass toward the foothills."

Steinbeck country continues farther west, beyond the Salinas River—that "slender stream, that twisted back and forth in its broad bed of gray sand," as Steinbeck writes in *East of Eden*—and across what some call the "lettuce curtain" that divides the hurting city of Salinas from tourist-friendly Monterey, just twenty miles away.

"Cannery Row in Monterey in California is a poem, a stink, a grating noise, a quality of light, a tone, a habit, a nostalgia, a dream," reads the opening sentence of Steinbeck's 1945 novel about the strip of fish-packing facilities that at its height processed one billion sardines every year. The industry began collapsing soon after Steinbeck published his novel, done in by overfishing. Within the author's lifetime, however, the town began converting the street into a tourist destination—cleaned-up and prettified, it was no longer stinky or grating, at least not in any way offensive to the senses. "They fish for tourists now, not pilchards," Steinbeck wrote in *Travels with Charley*. "And that

species they are not likely to wipe out." Little did he know!

WHERE TO VISIT

National Steinbeck Center
1 Main Street
Salinas, CA 93901

http://www.steinbeck.org

The Steinbeck House Restaurant
132 Central Avenue
Salinas, CA 93901

http://www.steinbeckhouse.com

Cannery Row
Monterey, CA 93940

https://canneryrow.com

In 1914, the poet **Robinson Jeffers** and his wife, Una, moved to Carmel-by-the-Sea, on the coast just south of Monterey. Thus the couple arrived "without knowing it to their inevitable place," as Jeffers later wrote. They lived in a small log cabin and went for long walks on a wild, unsettled property near Carmel Point. Five years later, Jeffers hired a local stonemason to help him build a house on the bluff using rocks from the craggy shoreline, as well as a few stray pieces, like a block of Hawaiian lava and a part of the Great Wall of China.

Tor House, poet Robinson Jeffers's self-designed home on the edge of a cliff in Carmel-by-the-Sea.

Over the years Jeffers welcomed many famous visitors to Tor House, including Charlie Chaplin, Charles Lindbergh, Sinclair Lewis, Edna St. Vincent Millay, Ansel Adams, Edgar Lee Masters, and Langston Hughes.

Jeffers would write in the morning while in the afternoon he turned his attention to working on the house itself, including a forty-foot tower he built for Irish-born Una in the style of her homeland's ancient Celtic architecture. Jeffers always worked with his hands and never used electric tools. He had a skill, as he wrote in his poem "Tor House," "to make stone love stone."

Tor House, run by a private foundation set up in Jeffers's honor, is now one of the most popular destinations in the Carmel area. Lining the walls in the house are the odds and ends Jeffers collected, including narwhal tusks and French guns. Visitors can stop on the ground floor of the tower to check out the poet's writing desk—and even sit in his chair—and then climb the narrow staircase for a 360-degree glimpse of the heart-stopping view. It has changed considerably since the poet's death in 1962. Late in life, Jeffers had to sell some of the surrounding property of the house. What was once a remote area is now crammed in with houses belonging to the wealthy—overdevelopment of the kind Jeffers bemoaned, and which has largely driven working-class artists from the area that was once a vibrant creative community.

Jeffers wrote about Tor House and its vicinity in many poems, letters, and other works. "Here was life purged of its ephemeral accretions," Jeffers recalled, in 1938, of his first seeing the area. "Men were riding after cattle, or plowing the headland, hovered by white seagulls, as they have done for thousands of years, and will for thousands of years to come. Here was contemporary life that was also permanent life." That same year, in a poem titled "Carmel Point," he described the importance of the house and its location to his elemental worldview:

> *We must uncenter our minds from ourselves;*
> *We must unhumanize our views a little,*
> *   and become confident*
> *As the rock and ocean that we were made*
> *   from.*

WHERE TO VISIT

Tor House
26304 Ocean View Avenue
Carmel-by-the-Sea, CA 93923

http://www.torhouse.org/

In 1940, the writer **Henry Miller** returned from many years in Europe and hit the road for a long car journey that he described in a cantankerous road-trip book, *The Air-Conditioned Nightmare* (1945). Miller was frustrated that his books were still considered too obscene to be published in his native country. He tried to live in Los Angeles for a time, but found the place unstimulating. After visiting a friend in Big Sur, the remote mountainous region on the coast south of Carmel-by-the-Sea, Miller was impressed by the "grandeur and eloquent silence," and decided to move there permanently.

Certainly, it couldn't have been more different from his native Brooklyn. The author paid $10 a month in rent for his cabin on Partington Ridge. Back then the region was extraordinarily remote—less than a hundred people lived along a stretch of seventy miles of coastline, and landslides often washed out the coastal road. He wrote to his friend Anaïs Nin that in Big Sur he could live "completely out of the world."

In 1957, Miller published *Big Sur and the Oranges of Hieronymus Bosch*, an homage to his adopted home. In addition to the usual mélange of idiosyncratic personal opinions boldly stated, rich descriptions, and quasi-mystical meditations, much of the book describes the history and geography and people of Big Sur. "On soft Spring nights I'll stand in the yard under the stars," he wrote. "Something good will come out of all things yet—And it will be golden and eternal just like that—There's no need to say another word."

People flocked to places like Big Sur, he wrote, because they discovered "that the American Way of Life is an illusory kind of existence, that the price demanded for the security and abundance it pretends to offer is too great."

Especially after he published the book, Miller's formerly isolated place in Big Sur became a popular destination for literary pilgrims. While staying in a borrowed cabin just up the coast, Jack Kerouac tried to visit Miller; but the meeting had to be canceled because Kerouac got too drunk; the younger Beat writer published his own book about the area, *Big Sur*, in 1962. Finally, Miller got tired of all the attention. "The people I couldn't abide," he later recalled, "were the visitors, the ones who came from nowhere and everywhere to analyze, to ask silly questions, or to discuss burning topics of no consequence. It's true, I must admit, that I myself was largely responsible for the invasion of these idiots. Had I not written about Big Sur no one would have been the wiser." He finally left and returned to Los Angeles, both to get away from the visitors and to be closer to his kids.

After Miller's death in 1980, his good friend Emil White, who moved to Big Sur at the same time he did, gave up his own home in a grove of towering redwoods to establish a Henry Miller Memorial Library, complete with photos of the author and paintings by him, plus letters and first editions of his works. Once asked why he surrendered his own residence for a shrine to Miller, White answered, "Because I missed him."

The Bixby Creek Bridge on Highway 1 in Big Sur–a landmark on the breathtaking road along the California coast.

An installation at the Henry Miller Memorial Library near the author's former home in Big Sur.

Ironically, as the library's own website acknowledges, Miller was not one who believed in memorials. He once wrote that they "defeated the purpose of a man's life. Only by living your own life to the full can you honor the memory of someone." Still, the library is a great place to relax by the fire with a cup of tea and a book, and take in the Big Sur sights and sounds. Gather strength for a walk up the hillside. "This," Miller wrote in *Big Sur*, "is the face of the Earth as the creator intended it to look."

WHERE TO VISIT

Henry Miller Memorial Library
48603 Highway 1
Big Sur, CA 93920

https://henrymiller.org

One cloudy October morning, in the opening scene of **Raymond Chandler**'s first novel, *The Big Sleep*, the philosophically minded, Camel-smoking, chess-playing detective Philip Marlowe shows up at a gloomy-looking mansion in Beverly Hills owned by an aging millionaire named General Sternwood. Impressed by the house's soaring entrance hall, massive fireplaces, and black-and-white tiled floors, Marlowe feels glad to have dressed up for the occasion. "I was neat, clean, shaved and sober, and I didn't care who knew it," he says. "I was everything the well-dressed private detective ought to be. I was calling on four million dollars."

The job promises good money, but it won't be easy. Along the way to cracking the case Sternwood is paying him for—dealing with the rare-books dealer who seems to be blackmailing the general's daughter—Marlowe finds himself ensnared in a convoluted web of

Greystone Mansion in Beverly Hills was Chandler's model for the Sternwood place in *The Big Sleep*—and has since served as the set for innumerable films.

pornographers, floozies, bootleggers, henchmen, and gamblers. The novel will take him on a tour of Los Angeles's seedy underworld, but it's the Sternwood place that captures Marlowe's—and the reader's—attention:

> Over the entrance doors, which would have let in a troop of Indian elephants, there was a broad stained-glass panel showing a knight in dark armor rescuing a lady who was tied to a tree and didn't have any clothes on but some very long and convenient hair. The knight had pushed the vizor of his helmet back to be sociable, and he was fiddling with the knots on the ropes that tied the lady to the tree and not getting anywhere. I

stood there and thought that if I lived in the house, I would sooner or later have to climb up there and help him. He didn't seem to be really trying.

Chandler based the Sternwood place on the sixty-seven-room Greystone Mansion at the end of Loma Vista Drive and a long driveway winding up the hillside. It has loomed above Beverly Hills since 1928, when an early Los Angeles oil tycoon named Edward L. Doheny presented it as a wedding gift for his son. Designed by the architect of the Hoover Dam and the downtown *Los Angeles Times* building, the Greystone place boasts walls of Indiana limestone three feet thick, and a roof of Vermont slate. The mansion cost so much to build that, if constructed today, it would be one of the most expensive pieces of real estate in southern California.

Its history is as dark as its vibe, featuring just the kind of strange, unsolved tale that would have attracted Chandler's attention. Just months after moving into the new mansion with his wife, the heir for whom it was built was shot dead in an apparent murder-suicide by his assistant. An *apparent* murder-suicide, please note: Some said the murderer may have been the heir, or even a different party. Nobody really knows for sure. The bodies were buried quickly, before autopsies could be performed. It was a mystery only a detective of Marlowe's caliber could have solved.

The heir's wife lived in the house for another twenty-five years before selling it in the 1950s once her children had moved out. Greystone was very nearly destroyed to build a subdivision, but the city of Beverly Hills bought it and opened the grounds as a park. Concerts are staged in the courtyard and the park hosts regular flower and garden festivals.

The Greystone Mansion is often used as a filming location. David Lynch's *Eraserhead* was filmed in the property's sixteen-thousand-square-foot stables. The famous bowling alley scene in *There Will Be Blood*—"I…drink…your…*milk shake*! THLUUUPP! I drink it up!"—was filmed in the basement. (Daniel Day-Lewis's character, like the mansion's original owner, was an oil man; Chandler, too, worked for an oil company before he took up fiction.) And the interior scenes for the reclusive tycoon's mansion in the Coen brothers' *The Big Lebowski*—inspired in part by *The Big Sleep* and other Chandler tales—was filmed at Greystone.

Even today it's easy to picture what made Chandler think Greystone would be the perfect setting for his noir novel. At the end of the story, Marlowe is back where he began, outside the Sternwood place. He drives off, back toward the city, thinking to himself, "What did it matter where you lay once you were dead? In a dirty sump or in a marble tower on top of a high hill? You were dead, you were sleeping the big sleep."

For other Chandler-related spots in Los Angeles—and there are many—a company called Esotouric offers a guided tour of locations from the author's life and work. Local publisher Herb Lester Associates also offers an official Raymond Chandler Map of Los Angeles.

WHERE TO VISIT

Greystone Mansion
905 Loma Vista Drive
Beverly Hills, CA 90210
https://www.greystonemansion.org

A Haunt of Ancient Peace

Anne of Green Gables, by L. M. Montgomery
Prince Edward Island, Canada

Few novels dominate the economy of the region they represent in fiction as thoroughly as *Anne of Green Gables*, which, more than a century after its publication, continues to define how Canada's Prince Edward Island presents itself to the outside world. In the novel, a white farmhouse in the bucolic province is home to an eleven-year-old orphan named Anne Shirley, the voluble redhead mistakenly sent to live with a middle-aged duo, Matthew and Marilla Cuthbert, brother and sister, who had hoped to adopt a boy to help them on their farm. Outspoken, armed with an active imagination, Anne is irresistible. (No less an authority than Mark Twain called her "the dearest and most lovable child in fiction since the immortal Alice.") The two of them take kindly to the girl and decide to let her stay.

Anne Shirley's famous house with the green-gabled roof, which belonged to relatives of author L. M. Montgomery.

The iconic home is now a well-visited museum.

An instant best seller when it was published in 1908, *Anne of Green Gables* has sold fifty million copies and been translated into some three dozen different languages. It's one of the most widely adored English-language books, not only in Canada but in the world.

Its author, Lucy Maud Montgomery, grew up in the town of Cavendish, on the northern part of Prince Edward Island. She was raised by her maternal grandparents after her mother died of tuberculosis and her father took off for Saskatchewan. In writing the novel, Montgomery changed the town's name to Avonlea, and located the story in a neighboring farmhouse owned by some cousins, a brother-sister pair like the one in the book. Three years after it was published, Montgomery married and moved to Ontario. She never returned to live on Prince Edward Island, though she set all but one of her twenty novels in the area where she had been raised. When she died in 1942 at the age of sixty-seven, the author was buried in the local Cavendish cemetery.

One reason Montgomery's novel is so revered is the evocative description of the island's landscape, colored "ruby, and emerald, and sapphire," surrounded by the Gulf of St. Lawrence, and of Anne's home, that "haunt of ancient peace," as the author writes, quoting Alfred, Lord Tennyson.

Prince Edward Island has capitalized on the *Anne* connection and then some. The young heroine's visage used to be found on provincial license plates, while the house that inspired her story became part of a national park in 1937. Its rooms have been outfitted to exactly match descriptions from the book, down to subtle details like a black shawl casually thrown over a bed. It receives tens of thousands of visitors every year, many of whom are from Japan, where the story has long been a smash hit under the somewhat less sonorous title *Red-haired Anne*. When the house partially burned down in the 1990s, Japanese readers helped raise funds to restore it. (For those Japanese readers unable to travel halfway around the world to get their Green Gables fill, a replica has been built in the Canadian World theme park in the small city of Ashibetsu.) Some couples travel to Prince Edward Island to get married on the grounds of Green Gables. Other visitors dress up as Anne, wearing straw hats with fake red braids poking out underneath.

While the inside of the house has been "preserved" to fit the novel, outside on the grounds the story is somewhat different. There, farmland has been replaced by a golf course.

Yet not all traces of Anne's world have been erased: a well-maintained trail runs through Balsam Hollow, the "Haunted Wood" from the book, to the remains of the Montgomery home, where the author penned *Anne* at the age of thirty-one, looking out her window over the hills and fields as the sunlight dimmed at end of day. Neglected for years, all that's left now is a stone foundation. Yet it's still possible to see Montgomery's precious view of the Gulf of St. Lawrence, which she described elsewhere as "a tiny blue gap between distant hills."

There are other *Anne*-related attractions scattered throughout the island. In Charlottetown, the provincial capital, a local arts center has put on a musical version of the story every summer for the last half-century—a Guinness world record. Avonlea Village, a local theme park, harkens back to the Prince Edward Island of Montgomery's time and allows visitors to dress in costumes inspired by the world of the novel. The author's birthplace in the town of New London, just a few miles away, is open to visitors. And the Anne of Green Gables Museum in nearby Park Corner occupies the home of Montgomery's Campbell family relatives on a 110-acre spread that the author used in other works. On display are a bookcase mentioned in *Anne of Green Gables* and Montgomery's homemade "crazy quilt," a mishmash of sharp shapes and vibrant colors. It was there at the Campbell home that Montgomery was married, in 1911.

Couples today who get married on the property use the same organ and furnishings that Montgomery had at her own nuptials.

"Kindred spirits are not so scarce as I used to think," Anne remarks at one point in the novel. "It's splendid to find out there are so many of them in the world."

WHERE TO VISIT

Green Gables Heritage Place
8619 Route 6
Cavendish, Prince Edward Island C0A 1M0
Canada

https://www.pc.gc.ca/en/lhn-nhs/pe
/greengables

The Haunting of Kingston Penitentiary

Alias Grace, by Margaret Atwood
Kingston, Ontario, Canada

In July 1843, in Upper Canada (present-day Ontario), the badly mutilated bodies of a well-off Scottish-born farmer named Thomas Kinnear and his pregnant housekeeper, Nancy Montgomery, were found in the cellar of his rural farmhouse not far outside Toronto. Two servants were also discovered missing—both Irish immigrants: sixteen-year-old Grace Marks and twenty-year-old James McDermott—as were some items from the house. Later the pair were tracked down in Lewiston, New York, across Lake Erie. Hauled back for a sensational trial, he was convicted of murder and executed; she was pronounced guilty of aiding and abetting the crime, but her death sentence was commuted to life in prison on account of her

age. Grace Marks, still a teenager, entered the grim dungeons of the fortress-like Kingston Penitentiary, fully expecting never to see the outside world again.

As a student at Harvard in the early 1960s, Ottawa native Margaret Atwood read an account of the Grace Marks case in *Life in the Clearing*, a memoir by the nineteenth-century Ontario pioneer Susanna Moodie. The story haunted her for years: In 1970, Atwood published a book of poetry based on Moodie's work, and a few years later wrote a play called *The Servant Girl* (a performance of which was filmed by the CBC). But the tale of Kinnear's murder continued to tug at her, and in 1996 Atwood returned to it in her ninth novel, *Alias Grace*. The tale begins in 1859, when Grace Marks has been in prison for fifteen years. She tells her life story to Dr. Simon Jordan, a young

The eerie Kingston Penitentiary, built in 1835.

physician hired to investigate whether the convicted murderess suffered from hysteria.

In 2016, Netflix turned the novel into a six-part miniseries. It was filmed on location at the actual Kingston Penitentiary, which has a colorful history even apart from its connections to the Kinnear case. The prison opened in 1835, making it several decades older than Canada itself. During his 1842 tour of North America, Charles Dickens visited the institution, which he called "well and wisely governed, and excellently regulated, in every respect." In later years Kingston Penitentiary gained a more sinister reputation as a place known for harsh conditions and brutal physical punishment—it was reputed at one time to have held inmates as young as eight years old. In 1923, a *Toronto Star* beat reporter named Ernest Hemingway covered a jailbreak and the hunt for the escapees. ("Then in the dark there was a rush across the road…") The penitentiary closed in 2013 and is now open to the public for guided tours.

For a pleasant, less eerie place to visit related to the book, devoted Atwood fans can head to Richmond Hill, a northern suburb of Toronto. In 2009, the town opened Alias Grace Park, just one block from the spot where the murders occurred, as an homage to Atwood's novel. Its design reflects

The ominous building is now closed to prisoners but open to the public.

elements from the book: Statues and playground equipment evoke imagery from the early days of white settlement in southern Ontario, and different styles of quilt, which Atwood used for chapter titles, are sandblasted into the pavement of the park.

As for Grace Marks herself, she finally received a pardon in 1872 and left Kingston Penitentiary. Apparently, she headed for New York, as she had thirty years earlier, but after that she vanishes from the historical record. What role she really had in the murders is still debated. She took the secret to her grave.

WHERE TO VISIT

Kingston Penitentiary
560 King Street West
Kingston, ON K7L 4V7
Canada

https://www.kingstonpentour.com

Alias Grace Park
Richmond Hill, ON L4S 2T2
Canada

Toiling in Ontario's Literary Garden

The Fiction of Alice Munro
Wingham, Ontario, Canada

In the small town of Wingham, in southwestern Ontario, under a sprawling catalpa tree in a former parking lot, the Alice Munro Literary Garden boasts a bower, flowerbeds, a curlicued archway, a statue of a young girl reading, and names of the beloved Canadian author's books inscribed on plaques embedded in the walkways.

Huron County, in southern Ontario, is Alice Munro country.

Built with money raised by locals, the garden is a destination for fans of the 2013 Nobel Prize winner who come to Wingham to get a glimpse of the world of Munro's fiction. As the Canadian writer Charles Foran once wrote in *The Walrus* magazine after visiting the town, "In the case of an artist like Alice Munro, so powerfully in touch with the interiority of lives that aren't often the stuff of fiction, the impulse to tour 'her' country may be especially strong: a Munro story can alert readers to complex truths about their own hearts, and about feelings for their own landscapes they were scarcely aware of."

Alice Ann Laidlaw was born in 1931 on a farm on the edge of Wingham, between the Maitland River and a cornfield, where her father raised foxes, mink, and turkeys. To her, the seemingly simple, unassuming Wingham was "the most interesting place in the world," as she once told the *New York Times*. Alice attended local public schools and published her first story in 1950 while still an undergraduate at the University of Western Ontario, in London, Ontario, an

The Alice Munro Literary Garden is on the grounds of the North Huron Museum.

hour and a half to the south. A year later she married a fellow student named James Munro and moved with him to British Columbia, first to West Vancouver and then to Victoria, where they opened a bookstore, Munro's Books. It's still around.

The job gave her time to read and write. In 1968, Munro published her first short story collection, *Dance of the Happy Shades*, which won her Canada's top literary prize, the Governor General's Award. She followed it four years later with a book of interconnected stories, *Lives of Girls and Women*. Later, the couple divorced and Munro returned to Huron County, where much of her work is set among the furrowed farmland, the tree breaks, the endless rows of corn. Marked by a sly and subtle simplicity of language, nonlinear chronologies, and a vivid evocation of Huron County, Munro's stories have earned the author high praise: She is "our Chekhov" (the writer Cynthia Ozick), and a "master of the contemporary short story" (the Nobel Prize committee).

In her fiction, Munro uses several different names as placeholders for Wingham: In different works it goes by Jubilee, Walley, Carstairs, and Hanratty. But all are clear stand-ins for Wingham, especially the poorer areas of Lower Town, where she was raised. "People's lives, in Jubilee as elsewhere, were dull, simple, amazing, and unfathomable—deep caves paved with kitchen linoleum," she wrote near the close of *Lives of Girls and Women*.

As in the case of Sauk Centre and Sinclair Lewis's *Main Street*, Wingham residents shuddered at Munro's stark, frank portrayal of the darker sides of the town's life: bootlegging, prostitution, and incest. She, too, has faced hostility. In 1980, the local paper published an editorial, titled "A Genius of Sour Grapes," complaining about Munro's "cruel" take on the town. After Munro won the Nobel in 2013, a *Toronto Star* reporter spoke with a descendant of the family whose tragic story— the death-by-scalding of a baby in the 1930s—featured in the plot of one of the author's early tales. After the story was published, a relative showed up at Munro's family farm and waved a shotgun, warning of dire consequences if she kept publishing such

trash. When the Literary Garden opened in 2002, Munro asked local police to guarantee her safety during the festivities. Years later, in an interview with the *Paris Review*, Munro blamed "the sex, the bad language, the incomprehensibility" of her novels for their poor reception in her hometown.

Unsurprisingly, given the Nobel, Wingham has been more willing of late to bask in the glow of its literary star. In addition to the garden, the town's North Huron Museum includes an exhibit about the author; a festival in her honor, once dormant, has come back to life. Munro spends much of the year in Clinton, a half-hour drive away.

In a brief 1974 essay, Munro recalled a seminal event from her childhood, the annual flooding of the Maitland River. "This ordinary place is sufficient," she wrote, "everything here is touchable and mysterious."

WHERE TO VISIT

Alice Munro Literary Garden
North Huron Museum
273 Josephine Street
Wingham, ON N0G 2W0
Canada

A Forest of Symbols in the Mexican Desert

Under the Volcano, by Malcolm Lowry
Cuernavaca, Morelos, Mexico

Malcolm Lowry's *Under the Volcano* (1947) often appears ranked among the top one hundred English-language novels of all time. Inspired in part by James Joyce's *Ulysses*, the book describes a period of twelve hours in the volcano-shadowed Mexican town of Quauhnahuac (the Aztec name for Cuernavaca, just south of Mexico City). It's a famously difficult read, with a meandering narrative structure and stream-of-consciousness narration, written in a dense, tangled style, filled with layered motifs—a whole "forest of symbols," as Lowry quotes Baudelaire in the novel. *Under the Volcano*, the critic D. T. Max once wrote in the *New Yorker*, is a book that "risks everything at every moment."

Lowry began working on it when he was living in Mexico while his first marriage was crumbling. The main character is a British

The eerie landscape of Mexico suffuses Lowry's magnum opus, a difficult but rewarding classic.

The Palace of Cortés in Cuernavaca, one of the oldest preserved buildings from the early colonial era in the Americas, sits on a hill overlooking the city.

consul just before the outbreak of the Second World War. With him are his partly estranged, soon-to-be ex-wife, Yvonne, and his half brother, Hugh. The action takes place on the Day of the Dead, November 2, 1938. The novel is as full of universal human experiences, like despair, disgrace, and self-destruction, as it is of Mexican history, geography, and politics.

The landscape of the place itself becomes a key character in the book. One passage in particular is striking, even haunting. Earnest, yearning Hugh and Yvonne, for whom he clearly has feelings, are weary from a long ride on horseback. They stop at a former imperial palace, looking out over the path they have just traveled, "over the plains, the scrub, the railway." Hugh rolls them cigarettes and they look out over the rocks and dunes and foothills and volcanoes as a storm gathers in the far distance. Lowry relates the scene from Hugh's perspective:

> There was something in the wild strength of this landscape, once a battlefield, that seemed to be shouting at him, a presence born of that strength whose cry his whole being recognized as familiar, caught and threw back into the wind, some youthful passage of courage and pride—the passionate, yet so nearly always hypocritical, affirmation of one's soul perhaps, he thought, of the desire to be, to do, good, what was right. It was as though he were gazing now beyond this expanse of plains and beyond the volcanoes out to the wide rolling blue ocean itself, feeling it in his heart still, the boundless impatience, the immeasurable longing.

During his time in the city, Lowry lived on Calle Humboldt, called Calle Nicaragua in the novel, though his biographers disagree on exactly which house was his. Later, Cuernavaca became a popular destination for Americans blacklisted from Hollywood during the 1950s. In 1984, John Huston filmed his adaptation of Lowry's novel on location. Malcolm Lowry drank himself to death at the age of forty-seven in 1957.

WHERE TO VISIT

Palace of Cortés
Calle Leyva 100,
Centro
Cuernavaca, Morelos 62000
Mexico

Calle Humboldt
Cuernavaca, Morelos 62448
Mexico

A Café Is a State of Mind

The Novels of Roberto Bolano
Mexico City, Mexico

In 2007, four years after his death from liver failure at the age of fifty, Roberto Bolano skyrocketed to literary fame with the publication in English of his sprawling road-trip story *The Savage Detectives*, which first came out in Spanish in 1999. The next year brought *2666*, the even more imposing twentieth-century epic of murder, breakdown, and degeneration.

Born in Bolivia, Bolano moved with his family to Mexico City in 1968. As a teenager, he dropped out of school and took up poetry

Café La Habana, the inspiration for Café Quito in *The Savage Detectives*.

and left-wing journalism. The home his family occupied stills stands, at Samuel 27 in Colonia Guadalupe Tepeyac. It's now occupied by a different family. Interviewed by a local journalist in 2013, they not only didn't know that Roberto Bolano had once lived in the house—they had no idea who he was.

While many places in Bolano's labyrinthine works can't be tracked to real-life antecedents, an exception is the legendary Café La Habana, thinly disguised in *The Savage Detectives* as Café Quito, a frequent meeting place for poets and other countercultural loiterers. Established in the early 1950s on a corner of Calle Bucareli, tucked into the voguish Colonia Juarez near the historical city center, Café Quito's formica countertops have over the years propped up

The café still plays host to important cultural events.

the coffee cups and notebooks of writers like Octavio Paz and Gabriel García Márquez; in the mid-1950s, expat rebels like Fidel Castro and Che Guevara supposedly frequented the café while planning the Cuban Revolution.

Café Quito is still there, a relatively untouched remnant of bygone days, and a vibrant forum for the capital's cultural scene. In 2017, it played host to a unique literary tribute by the American singer Patti Smith. Five years earlier, she had written a long poem called *Hecatomb*, based on the slaughter of one hundred oxen in Bolano's novel *Amulet*. For *Café La Habana Sessions*, Smith's two-week artist-residency/performance at the storied Mexico City establishment, she read from *Hecatomb* and performed some of her songs while surrounded by photographs she had taken over the years, including one of Roberto Bolano's writing chair at his final home, in Blanes, on the Catalonian coast. Smith's *La Habana* project, according to the organizer, local art exhibition space Sonora 128, was "inspired by the idea"—an idea

WHERE TO VISIT

Café La Habana
Esquina Fray Servando Teresa de Mier
Mexico City 06600
Mexico

with which Bolano undoubtedly would have agreed—"that a café is not a place, but a state of mind."

A Street of Strivers in Port of Spain

The Novels of V. S. Naipaul
Port of Spain, Trinidad

V. S. Naipaul, winner of the 2001 Nobel Prize in Literature, was known for giving a lighthearted, even comedic treatment to his stories of poverty and despair in his hometown of Port of Spain, Trinidad. Despite being impoverished British subjects in the Caribbean during World War II—and members of the Indo-Trinidadian subminority to boot—his characters insist on seeking a sense of dignity beyond despair.

In *Miguel Street*, his 1959 book of linked stories, Naipaul describes life on the street where he spent time living with relatives while growing up. It's based on Luis Street in Woodbrook, a section of Port of Spain. The colorful characters in the book, objects of both ridicule and admiration, partake in shenanigans like running illegal brothels, gambling, starting up sham schools, and making signs promoting businesses—tailoring and carpentry—even though they never do anything at all.

Many of the characters on Miguel Street are resigned to the conclusion that things will never really get better for them and their neighbors. Thus their constant drinking and violence (especially against women). "Well, what you expect in a place like this?" one character, Hat, asks when another, Big Foot, tries to make something of himself.

The people of Port of Spain, the capital of Trinidad and Tobago, gave Naipaul limitless material for his explorations of ambition, inertia, and the effects of colonialism.

Beneath the schemes, low expectations, and limited opportunities, however, is a desire to still find meaning and beauty in their beaten-down world. From an eccentric man on the street who calls himself "B. Wordsworth"—for "black" Wordsworth—the Naipaul-like narrator learns what it means to be an artist, and discovers that, unlike all the macho men on the block, "When you're a poet, you can cry for everything."

In Naipaul's next novel, the more famous *A House for Mr. Biswas* (1961), a man struggles all his life to transcend the unfortunate circumstances of his birth. Mahoun Biswas is born severely underweight and has six fingers on one hand—a sure sign of bad luck, according to his family. Later in life, Biswas is fired from his job as a journalist and has to move his family from one rented house to another.

Despite all this, however, Biswas is committed to the pursuit of happiness. "How terrible," he notes, "to have lived without even attempting to lay claim to one's portion of the earth; to have lived and died as one had been born, unnecessary and unaccommodated."

By the end of the story (which returns to the beginning), Biswas has finally achieved his dream of owning his own home. The house on Sikkim Street is so impressive a structure it "could be seen from two or three streets away and was known all over St. James [Naipaul's stand-in for Port of Spain]. It was like a huge and squat sentry-box: tall,

square, two-storeyed, with a pyramidal roof of corrugated iron." Biswas has succeeded in laying claim to his "portion of the earth." As the narrator of *Miguel Street* puts it, while many might look at the Trinidadian streets from the outside and say "Slum!…we who lived there saw our street as a world."

Mr. Biswas's house was based on the one at 26 Nepaul Street, in Port of Spain, where Naipaul lived with his parents before his move to Britain to study at Oxford. In 2013, the renovated structure opened to the public as the Naipaul House and Literary Museum; the bottom floor looks as it did in Naipaul's childhood. The Friends of Mr. Biswas, a nonprofit that owns the property, is collecting Naipaul-related memorabilia and restoring the outdoor gardens. Two apartments in the house are available for rent to scholars of Trinidadian culture.

WHERE TO VISIT

Naipaul House and Literary Museum
26 Nepaul Street
St. James
Port of Spain
Trinidad

http://www.friendsofmrbiswas.org/pages
/the-naipaul-house

EUROPE

Wentworth Woodhouse in South Yorkshire, one possible inspiration for Pemberley. The palace was reputed to be the finest house in England when it was finished in the mid-eighteenth century.

Elizabeth Bennet, Mistress of Pemberley

Pride and Prejudice, by Jane Austen
Derbyshire, England

Elizabeth Bennet, the outspoken heroine of one of Jane Austen's most celebrated works, the 1813 novel *Pride and Prejudice*, is often considered a kind of proto-feminist. Refusing to marry a man only for his property, wealth, and status—unlike most young women of the time—Elizabeth expresses a certain hostility toward the very wealthy yet egotistical Mr. Darcy. Having already rejected one

proposal from the suitor, Elizabeth is convinced he is not the man for her.

It's only when Elizabeth pays a visit to Mr. Darcy's estate, Pemberley, that she begins to see things differently. As she approaches the estate, her eye is "instantly caught by Pemberley House…a large, handsome stone building, standing well on rising ground, and backed by a ridge of high woody hills."

She is "delighted" by Pemberley's natural beauty. Unlike many stately houses of

The gardens of Wentworth Woodhouse.

the time, which Elizabeth thought were marred by too many "fine carpets" and "satin curtains," Pemberley seems different: There, Austen has her reflect, it seemed that "natural beauty had been so little counteracted by an awkward taste." Like Darcy himself, the home had an unassuming beauty, unadorned by the niceties and trappings of the age.

The observation triggers in Elizabeth the beginnings of a profound change of heart. It was "at this moment," Austen writes, "that

she felt that to be mistress of Pemberley might be something!"

Later in the novel, after Elizabeth finally agrees to marry Darcy, her sister Jane—who up to this point thought Elizabeth still hated Darcy—asks, "Will you tell me how long you have loved him?" Elizabeth replies, "It has been coming on so gradually, that I hardly know when it began. But I believe I must date it from my first seeing his beautiful grounds at Pemberley."

There are two main candidates for the

house in Britain. The family that owned it in Austen's time was the Fitzwilliam family—which also happens to be Mr. Darcy's first name.

The Jane Austen Society continues to insist that Chatsworth House must be the model for Pemberley, because the author seems never to have visited Wentworth Woodhouse. Austen scholar Janine Barchas, on the other hand, suggests that because Austen specifically mentions Chatsworth House by name in the novel—as a place where Elizabeth and some friends travel to visit—it can't, by the laws of literary geography, also be the basis for Pemberley. Wentworth was sold to a nonprofit trust in 2016 and is now open for public tours, as is Chatsworth House. Maybe someday a vote by *Pride and Prejudice* readers will decide the matter.

model on which Austen based her depiction of Pemberley. For years, scholars suggested the original was Chatsworth House, which, like the fictional version, is in the county of Derbyshire, and it was used as the setting for the 2005 film version starring Keira Knightley.

More recently, however, experts' opinion has shifted in favor of Wentworth Woodhouse in nearby South Yorkshire, even more impressive than Chatsworth: At 124,600 square feet, with some three hundred rooms, the seventeenth-century Wentworth estate was once named by Guinness the largest private

WHERE TO VISIT

Wentworth Woodhouse
Wentworth, Rotherham S62 7TQ
UK
https://www.wentworthwoodhouse.org.uk

Chatsworth House
Bakewell DE45 1PP
UK
https://www.chatsworth.org

A Mile-Long Trail for the Queen of Crime

The Novels of Agatha Christie
Torquay, England

Agatha Christie, the queen of crime, was born in the seaside town of Torquay, on the English Riviera. Fifteen of her more than sixty novels are set in the region, and several in Torquay itself, though it goes by different names in different books. Perhaps the most recognizable location in town connected with Christie's fictional universe is the Imperial Hotel, constructed in 1866, high on a cliff with gorgeous views over Torbay. The Imperial, thinly disguised as the Majestic Hotel, appears in *Peril at End House* (1932) and *The Body in the Library* (1942), and as itself in the final chapter of *Sleeping Murder* (1976), Christie's last novel, published nine months after her death in 1976 at the age of eighty-five.

Torquay has done an exceptional job tending to the legacy of its most famous native. In 1990, to mark the centennial of Christie's birth, a handmade bronze bust of the author was unveiled by her daughter. It's just one stop

The stretch of coastal villages along Torbay is often known as the English Riviera.

on the Agatha Christie Mile, which takes visitors on a short walking tour of sites important to the novelist's life and work—the church where she was baptized, the Victorian-era Princess Gardens where she loved to stroll, the pier where she roller-skated, the classy Pavilion theater where her husband proposed to her after a Wagner concert, the Grand Hotel where the couple spent their honeymoon, the cavern from *The Man in the Brown Suit* (1924), and the railway station where, during the 1990 centennial celebrations, two people dressed up as Christie's most famous characters, the mustachioed Belgian detective Hercule Poirot and Miss Marple, the spinster-investigator,

Top: Archie Christie proposed to Agatha Miller at the Pavilion theater in 1913. Bottom: Several of Agatha Christie's novels are set in Torquay, the seaside town where she was born in 1890.

met—unlike in the books, where their creator ensured they never did.

Every September, Torquay hosts an annual International Agatha Christie Festival, with tea parties, film screenings, talks, plays, refreshments, and period-dress parties. At the Torquay Museum, the Agatha Christie Gallery features exhibits related to Christie's life and work and her relationship to the region, as well as a replica of Poirot's London flat from televised adaptations, props and costumes used in the filming, and some of Christie's own handwritten notes and first editions of her novels.

WHERE TO VISIT

The Imperial Torquay
Parkhill Road
Torquay TQ1 2DG
UK

http://www.theimperialtorquay.co.uk

Torquay Museum
529 Babbacombe Road
Torquay TQ1 1HG
UK

http://www.torquaymuseum.org
/homepage

Top Withens, a sixteenth-century farmhouse, may have inspired the windswept home featured in *Wuthering Heights*.

The View from the Heath

Wuthering Heights, by Emily Brontë
West Yorkshire, England

"This is certainly a beautiful country!" Mr. Lockwood, a visitor up from London, writes in his journal. "In all England, I do not believe that I could have fixed on a situation so completely removed from the stir of society."

Indeed he could not have. As the back-story of Wuthering Heights, hilltop home of the Lockwoods' landlord—the strange, tortured Heathcliff—unfolds over the next few hundred pages, the house itself emerges almost as a character in the novel, as well as the unforgettable setting of one of the most devastating love stories in literature. It is as brooding and isolated, and yet also as strangely appealing, as the hero himself.

Wuthering Heights, Emily Brontë's first and only novel, was published in 1847 under the pseudonym Ellis Bell. The author tragically died the following year, at just thirty years old; her health was probably compromised by the same harsh climate that so fascinated her and inspired her work. In 1850, her sister Charlotte shepherded a second edition into print. The novel immediately captured attention in the English-speaking literary world, alternately praised for its brilliance and

High Sunderland Hall, a manor house built in 1600, was demolished in 1951.

originality and condemned for its bleakness and alleged misanthropy.

There is no real place called Wuthering Heights. As Lockwood reports, the name was taken from "a significant provincial adjective, descriptive of the atmospheric tumult to which its station is exposed, in stormy weather"—all of which is to say, in the urban sophisticate's parlance, that up on the moors it's really, really windy.

According to Ellen Nussey, a lifelong friend of the Brontës, Emily's inspiration for the house was Top Withens, a late-sixteenth-century farmhouse on a hilltop three miles outside Haworth, the small mill town where the sisters grew up. (The parsonage where they lived—their father was the local priest—is now a museum run by the Brontë Society.) Top Withens was inhabited well into the

twentieth century, but it was later abandoned and now is open to the elements—the roof gone, the thick stone walls beginning to crumble. The house is a popular walking destination from nearby Haworth. The trail even takes visitors past a waterfall that was a favorite spot for the Brontë sisters. In a letter, Charlotte called it "a perfect torrent racing over the rocks, white and beautiful!"

The only problem with the Top Withens theory, however, is that even when it stood the house looked nothing like the description of Wuthering Heights. The truth is that its grounds probably inspired only the setting for the house, the "bleak, hilly coal country" described in the novel.

The mansion that was the model for the peculiar, harrowing exterior of Wuthering Heights was probably a place called High

Sunderland Hall, which was very near the school where Emily Brontë once served as a teacher. In the first chapter of *Wuthering Heights*, Mr. Lockwood describes "a quantity of grotesque carving" over the doors of the house—a "wilderness of crumbling griffins and shameless little boys." High Sunderland had precisely such adornments, as well as Latin inscriptions, like *fama virtutum tuba perennis*: "The fame of virtue is an eternal trumpet."

Sadly, unlike the ruins at Top Withens, High Sunderland can no longer be visited. Structurally compromised by nearby mining operations, it was demolished in 1951. Yet the bizarre sculptures and intricate stonework that probably inspired Brontë's fictional Wuthering Heights can still be seen

WHERE TO VISIT

Top Withens
Hebden Bridge
West Yorkshire HX7 8RP
UK

Shibden Hall
Lister's Road
Halifax HX3 6XG
UK

http://museums.calderdale.gov.uk/visit
/shibden-hall

on the grounds of a neighboring house, the early fifteenth-century Shibden Hall, which is open to the public.

Tranquility Along the River Wye

"Lines Composed a Few Miles Above…Tintern Abbey," by William Wordsworth
Tintern, Wales

The oldest buildings of Tintern Abbey, on the Welsh side of the River Tye that separates Wales and England, were put up in the twelfth century by Cistercian monks. Also known as Trappists, the Cistercians were (and are) a particularly austere sect of friars who emphasized chastity, silence, prayer, manual labor, and economic self-sufficiency. (They are still known for brewing especially tasty beers.)

Over the course of a few hundred years, the abbey was expanded and rebuilt in a hodgepodge of medieval architectural styles. Most of the multicolored sandstone church that survives today was consecrated in 1301. Later, the abbey suffered badly from the Black Death, and from Welsh uprisings against English rule. During the

The ruins of Tintern Abbey evoked in Wordsworth feelings of tranquility, harmony, and "unremembered pleasure."

conversion of England to Protestantism under King Henry VIII in the sixteenth century, all the monasteries were dissolved and abandoned. The Crown took over nearly one thousand former Catholic properties (many with hundreds of resident monks and nuns), seized their prized artifacts for the state, and auctioned off the lands. The lead in Tintern Abbey's roof was sold and the buildings reduced to ruins, the soaring arches covered with ivy as time and nature had their way.

In the mid-eighteenth century, a new travel trend arose in England as people began to visit wild, remote parts of the British Isles and the ruins of castles and churches from days gone by. Travel writers and painters (like Thomas Gainsborough and J. M. W. Turner) journeyed through the Wye Valley and spread the word of Tintern Abbey's enchanting air of forsaken wonders.

In 1793, a young poet named William Wordsworth visited Tintern Abbey for the first time. It made quite an impression. He had just returned from revolutionary France, where he had supported the declaration of the Republic, fathered an illegitimate child, and barely escaped the turmoil of the Reign of Terror. His trip to Wales was part of an intentional turn away from politics and a return to the simpler pleasures of his youth: forests, valleys, mountains, and streams.

Five years later, on a walking tour with his sister, Dorothy, Wordsworth returned to the abbey and wrote a poem about it: "Lines Written (or Composed) a Few Miles above Tintern Abbey, on Revisiting the Banks of the Wye during a Tour, July 13, 1798." It was later published in *Lyrical Ballads*, a collection coauthored with his friend Samuel Taylor Coleridge, that skyrocketed both of them to literary stardom and inaugurated a new era for English letters.

Wordsworth's poem is a 159-line meditation on the strange, silent effect that the memory of his first visit had had on him in the intervening years, even when he wasn't consciously aware of it:

> *These beauteous forms,*
> *Through a long absence, have not been to me*
> *As is a landscape to a blind man's eye:*
> *But oft, in lonely rooms, and 'mid the din*
> *Of towns and cities, I have owed to them,*
> *In hours of weariness, sensations sweet,*
> *Felt in the blood, and felt along the heart;*
> *And passing even into my purer mind*
> *With tranquil restoration:—feelings too*
> *Of unremembered pleasure: such, perhaps,*
> *As have no slight or trivial influence*
> *On that best portion of a good man's life,*
> *His little, nameless, unremembered, acts*
> *Of kindness and of love.*

The very thought of what he saw, heard, and felt is enough to make him want to be a better person. Yet the memory has had the even deeper effect, the poet goes on to say, of lightening the burden of the mystery and turbulence of life, of reconciling him to the inevitability of death, when

> *with an eye made quiet by the power*
> *Of harmony, and the deep power of joy,*
> *We see into the life of things.*

Whenever he needs to remind himself of those realizations, those commitments, all

The abbey fell into disrepair nearly 500 years ago.

he has to do is think back to what he saw those years ago in the Welsh borderlands:

> *How oft, in spirit, have I turned to thee,*
> *O sylvan Wye! thou wanderer thro' the*
>   *woods,*
> *How often has my spirit turned to thee!*

Even now, on his return visit, Wordsworth takes pleasure in the thought that his mind, like a busy squirrel, is packing away "life and food / For future years."

Strangely enough, Wordsworth says nothing in the poem about the abbey itself, though the imposing, ponderous ruins are its animating spirit, and the meditations they inspire—on morality and mortality—are its central concern. One reason, perhaps, is that the area around the abbey had become heavily industrialized in recent years and was, as one scholar puts it, "a dwelling-place of beggars and the wretchedly poor." So the abbey's reality didn't exactly correspond with Wordsworth's rhapsodies on the blissful purity of nature. But that didn't make them any less true.

Tourism to Tintern Abbey has only grown since Wordsworth's day, aided by the

WHERE TO VISIT

Tintern Abbey
Monmouthshire, Wales NP16 6SE
UK

https://cadw.gov.wales/daysout
/tinternabbey/?lang=en

Keeping up the long tradition of artists making pilgrimages to Tintern Abbey, Allen Ginsberg visited the abbey in the summer of 1967. He dropped acid and wrote a poem, "Wales Visitation," which he read on television, with adorable earnestness and wild gesticulations, to a kindly, condescending William F. Buckley, smiling through pursed lips:

> …& the silent thought of Wordsworth in eld Stillness
>
> Clouds passing through skeleton arches of Tintern Abbey–
>
> Bard Nameless as the Vast, Babble to Vastness!

"I kinda like that," Buckley said when Ginsberg stopped reading.

arrival of rail service to the Tintern area near the end of the nineteenth century. The ruins were purchased by the Crown in 1901, thereafter intensively repaired and partially reconstructed. In 1984, the grounds were taken over by Cadw, the Welsh heritage-tourism agency. Now some seventy thousand people visit it every year, including three incredibly lucky artists-in-residence. Nearby, the newly renovated Anchor Inn incorporates the original cider mill of Tintern Abbey and a thirteenth-century archway that carried water from the church buildings to the Wye.

The George, an inn on Southwark's Talbot Square, evokes the feeling of the long-demolished Tabard, where Chaucer's Canterbury-bound travelers begin their pilgrimage.

London Through the Ages

Geoffrey Chaucer, Charles Dickens, Virginia Woolf, George Orwell, J. K. Rowling, Zadie Smith, Poets' Corner

It's April of 1387. Our narrator has fallen in with a motley assortment of pilgrims— "nyne and twenty in a compaignye"—at the Tabard Inn, in Southwark, just outside London, where popular pastimes like prostitution and bear-baiting are legal, making for a lively entertainment district for those from the capital. The Tabard, however, is also a common resting place for travelers heading down the ancient Roman road to coastal Dover, or, closer, to Canterbury, to pay their respects at the tomb of the martyred twelfth-century archbishop, Thomas Becket.

In **Geoffrey Chaucer**'s *Canterbury Tales*, the Tabard serves as the setting of the prologue, in which each character is introduced and the inn's proprietor, Harry Bailey, suggests the narrative competition that leads to the twenty-two stories presented in the rest of the book.

Established in 1307, the Tabard Inn was destroyed in a late seventeenth-century inferno; the inn was swiftly rebuilt and opened as the Talbot. Under that name, it flourished for two centuries more until the old path was bypassed by the railroad. Near the spot, in today's Talbot Square (not far from Renzo Piano's controversial ninety-five-floor skyscraper, the Shard), there's a plaque commemorating the Tabard and its connection to Chaucer. Also nearby is the George—a quaint pub dating nearly to the time of Chaucer (it was rebuilt after the same fire that destroyed the Tabard). Shakespeare, too, supposedly slugged pints there—as, in its current incarnation, did Charles Dickens.

WHERE TO VISIT

The George Inn
77 Borough High Street
London SE1 1NH
UK
https://www.greeneking-pubs.co.uk/pubs/
greater-london/george-southwark/

Few authors are as closely associated with a city as **Charles Dickens** is with London, the bustling, often grimy setting for almost all his major works. Born in Portsmouth, the author knew his adopted hometown as well as anyone ever has. He used to love walking the streets, especially after dark; on some nights he covered as many as ten or twelve miles. As a child he moved to the Southwark area of the city, and when his father was thrown in nearby Marshalsea prison as a debtor, Dickens, just twelve years old, had to go work in a shoe-blacking factory on the site of today's Charing Cross railway station. Years later, he used Southwark as the setting for *Little Dorrit*, especially the prison and the Church of St. George the Martyr, which today has a stained-glass window depicting the book's main character.

Many spots in London recur throughout Dickens's fifteen beloved novels and numerous other works of fiction and journalism. The bustling, crime-ridden market at Covent Garden, for instance, appears in both *The Pickwick Papers* and *Oliver Twist*, while Arthur Clennam from *Little Dorrit* lives in a dingy flat in the area and Lady Dedlock from *Bleak House* dies of exposure at the grave of her former fiancé in a nearby cemetery (since made into a playground). In his first book, the miscellaneous collection of short pieces titled *Sketches by Boz*, Dickens described the pavement of the market in the morning as "strewed

The Holborn home, where the author lived for two and a half years and where he wrote *Oliver Twist,* is a museum.

with decayed cabbage-leaves, broken hay-bands…men are shouting, carts backing, horses neighing, boys fighting, basket-women talking, piemen expatiating on the excellence of their pastry, and donkeys braying."

As a young man Dickens worked as a clerk in the lawyer-heavy Temple neighborhood around the Inns of Court. Gray's Inn, one of the four legal associations in the vicinity, appears in *David Copperfield* and *The Pickwick Papers.* In *Great Expectations,* Pip is living in Fountain Court when a convict shows up with a secret that will change his life. Fountain

Court is also the setting of an important scene in *Martin Chuzzlewit,* when Dickens describes the inns this way: "There is yet a drowsiness in its courts and a dreamy dullness in its trees and gardens; those who pace its lanes and squares may yet hear the echoes of their footsteps on the sounding stones."

Near to the inns, surrounded by buildings of the London School of Economics, is the Old Curiosity Shop, which, though it probably did not in fact inspire Dickens's novel of the same name, does a brisk business trading on the misperception that it did. Dating to the mid-sixteenth century, built from the the discarded lumber of old ships, it's an intriguing place to visit nonetheless.

Near Camden, in southeastern London, there's the formerly squalid slum of Saffron Hill, where Fagin, the slimy pickpocketers' leader in *Oliver Twist,* keeps his sordid lair, "a dirty and wretched place," on Field Lane. This is where the Artful Dodger first takes Oliver when they meet. "The street was very narrow and muddy, and the air was impregnated with filthy odours," Dickens writes.

For the genuine experience of Dickens's London, of course, a visit to a suitably ancient and atmospheric pub is essential, and while many in London claim the author sipped a pint here or there, the consensus claim for the most Dickensian choice is Ye Olde Cheshire Cheese, dating from 1667 (just after the devastating fire), near the onetime newspaper row on Fleet Street. Mentioned in *A Tale of Two Cities*, the Cheshire Cheese has literary associations beyond Dickens: Visited by the likes of Mark Twain; G. K. Chesterton; Alfred, Lord Tennyson; and Arthur Conan Doyle, the pub has also appeared in works by Robert Louis Stevenson and Anthony Trollope.

The ultimate Dickens haunt in London, of course, is his tastefully furnished house at 48 Doughty Street, where he lived while writing *Oliver Twist*, *The Pickwick Papers*, and *Nicholas Nickleby*. Some of his furnishings, clothing, and other memorabilia are on display there. The author, who died in 1870 at age fifty-eight, is buried in Poets' Corner in Westminster Abbey, surrounded by his fellow literary greats.

Platform 9¾ in King's Cross Station.

WHERE TO VISIT

Charles Dickens Museum
48 Doughty Street
London WC1N 2LX
UK
https://dickensmuseum.com

Of the many revelations that eleven-year-old Harry Potter—the namesake of **J. K. Rowling**'s record-breaking, history-making, devotion-inspiring children's fantasy series—unwittingly stumbles upon after receiving his admission letter from Hogwarts, the school of witchcraft and wizardry, is that the magical world he hopes to enter isn't in some far-off place, but that it exists, unseen, in the very London he has known all along.

The bookshops in charming Cecil Court.

To help Harry get his school supplies, Hagrid, the giant gamekeeper at Hogwarts, takes the confused young wizard to the Leaky Cauldron pub and inn, on Charing Cross Road. There, in a backroom, Hagrid taps a few bricks to access a portal into Diagon Alley, inspired by Cecil Court, near the Leicester Square station on the Tube. (Leadenhall market, in the City of London, was used for filming the Diagon scenes in the films.) One of the shops in Cecil Court, Watkins Books, claims to be the oldest purveyor of occult literature in the world.

Another major destination for *Potter* fans in the UK capital is Platform 9¾, where Harry is instructed to go in order to catch the express train to Hogwarts. It's in the real-life King's Cross Station. Today the King's Cross Station has a sign dedicated to the invisible platform—though it's really between platforms 4 and 5—with a hand-trolley lodged halfway through the brick wall Harry had to boldly crash through to get there. Nearby is a Potter-themed shop designed to look like Ollivanders, makers of fine wands since 382 BC.

WHERE TO VISIT

Platform 9¾ at King's Cross Station
Kings Cross
London N1 9AP
UK

Eric Blair was born in India in 1903, but he spent most of his life in London. After returning to England and attending Eton College, Blair served five years in the British colonial police force in Burma. He moved to London to become a writer and lived in an unheated attic apartment at 22 Portobello Road in Notting Hill. Some mornings the room was so cold he had to thaw his hands over a candle before beginning to write. Soon he was publishing essays, stories, and reviews in major magazines. By 1933, Blair adopted **George Orwell** ("a good round English name") as a pseudonym to prevent his family from suffering any embarrassment from his daring, radical work.

After many adventures—tramping in London and Paris, fighting in the Spanish Civil War—Orwell returned to London and lived in several different apartments. When one building was destroyed by German bombs, he moved to his final home, a fourth-floor flat at 27b Canonbury Square in now-chic Islington, then a derelict and working-class neighborhood. It was here that Orwell lived when he wrote his famous dystopian novel *1984*, which imagined London as the dark and stultifying metropolis of a tightly controlled surveillance state where the insidious meaninglessness of "doublethink"—alternative facts, fake news—had reduced the populace to a confused and divided underclass. The novel reimagined many London locations Orwell knew well: Trafalgar Square became Victory Square, with a monument to Big Brother rather than Nelson's Column in its center.

Orwell died one year after his novel was published and never lived to see his prophecy come true. But these days it isn't hard to see London as Orwell imagined it might become. In a city with millions of closed-circuit cameras, the average Londoner is caught on camera as many as 300 times every day. There are twenty-eight cameras within two hundred yards of his Islington flat. In 2017, a statue of Orwell—leaning forward, cigarette in hand, as if arguing a point—was installed outside Broadcasting House, the headquarters of the BBC and Orwell's model for the Ministry of Truth in *1984*. On a wall behind the statue is a line from Orwell's preface to his classic 1945 novella *Animal Farm*: "If liberty means anything at all, it means the right to tell people what they do not want to hear."

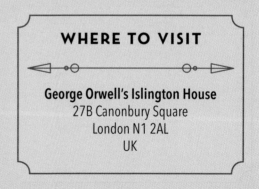

WHERE TO VISIT

George Orwell's Islington House
27B Canonbury Square
London N1 2AL
UK

It's a bright Wednesday in June, after the war, and London is looking vibrant, crowded, exquisite. The young wife is planning a party. She is going to buy the flowers herself.

What a morning! What a lark! Clarissa Dalloway leaves her house in Westminster and as she crosses Victoria Street is pleased to hear the chimes atop Parliament toll another passing hour. **Virginia Woolf**, the creator of this unforgettable day, plunges us into Clarissa's mind: "For having lived in Westminster—how many years now? over twenty—one feels even in the midst of the traffic, or waking at night, Clarissa was positive, a particular hush, or solemnity; an indescribable pause; a suspense (but that might be her heart, affected, they said, by influenza) before Big Ben strikes. There! Out it boomed. First a warning, musical; then the hour, irrevocable."

Clarissa loves walking the streets of London. They're better even, she tells her old friend Hugh Whitbread, whom she runs into at the entrance to St. James's Park ("the silence; the mist; the hum"), than the lanes and footpaths in the country.

"Did it matter then, she asked herself, walking towards Bond Street, did it matter that she must inevitably cease completely?"

Virginia Woolf was born Adeline Virginia Stephen in London in 1882 and lived there nearly all her life. Her birth home in Kensington still stands, near Royal Albert Hall. When she wrote *Mrs. Dalloway*, her fourth novel, in 1924, she had just moved with her husband Leonard to Tavistock Square after a brief time outside the city: She fed into the novel's pages her joy at returning to London's familiar streets. Woolf especially loved what she called "street-haunting," watching people move through the city—it was an inspiration for her writing and a consolation during her struggles with depression. Both the Tavistock Square home and a later one near Mecklenburgh Square were destroyed in the bombing of London during World War II, but by then the Woolfs were spending most of their time at Monk's House, their country retreat in East Sussex, where in 1941 the novelist tragically killed herself by drowning.

London is an ever-present backdrop for *Mrs. Dalloway*, full of reminders, from Buckingham Palace to the statues of famous conquerors in Trafalgar Square, of the rise and fall of empires and the passage of history—and the indifference such processes have toward the individual. The novel is laced with intensely florid descriptions of places notable precisely for their ordinariness: "Bond Street fascinated her; Bond Street early in the morning in the season; its flags flying; its shops; no

splash; no glitter; one roll of tweed in the shop where her father had bought his suits for fifty years; a few pearls; salmon on an ice-block."

Clarissa ends up, of course, at the florist, to place an order for the party. According to Woolf scholar Katherine Hill-Miller, Mulberry's was probably based on an outfit called G. Adam & Co., "florists and fruiterers to the King and Prince of Wales."

That's where the narrative first shifts to Septimus Warren Smith, the war veteran suffering from traumatic stress, whose London—not least because of his frequent hallucinations—looks a lot different from Mrs. Dalloway's.

Mrs. Dalloway's walk through London takes her past Big Ben.

For travelers looking to pay homage to Virginia Woolf and her most famous literary creation, there are a few options. The Woolfs' beloved Monk's House is open for tours, decorated, the website promises, "as if they just stepped out for a walk." In London itself the places are less official. A website called the Mrs. Dalloway Mapping Project makes it easy to follow each of the characters whose inner thoughts make up most of the novel. All of Woolf's former homes in London have blue plaques commemorating their connection to her. And a restaurant named Dalloway Terrace at the Bloomsbury Hotel offers afternoon tea. All that said, there's surely no better way to honor Woolf, and to see what she saw, than to do a little random street-haunting for yourself.

WHERE TO VISIT

Bond Street
London
UK

In 2000, at only twenty-four years old, **Zadie Smith** burst onto the literary scene with *White Teeth*, her first novel, a multigenerational coming-of-age tale set in Willesden, the vivid but struggling northwest London

neighborhood where she was raised. An often-ignored side of London, once heavily Irish but increasingly populated by immigrants from Africa and the Caribbean, Willesden is part of Brent, the most diverse borough in the entire United Kingdom. Living in the area, Smith once said, "You hear a lot of different voices all the time."

In *White Teeth*, Smith celebrates the neighborhood's shared sense of particularity and of place, a sense threatened by capitalism and political Thatcherism, with references to local spots like spacious Roundwood Park; Harlesden Clock, put up in 1888 to celebrate Queen Victoria's jubilee; and a neighborhood pub called the Spotted Dog—as Smith writes, "a famous Willesden landmark, described in 1792 as 'being a well accostomed Publick house.'"

Smith returned to the area in later works, most notably in *NW*, her 2012 novel named for the neighborhood's postal abbreviation. The book follows a set of Londoners who, after growing up in the same housing projects, followed very different paths in life. Each struggles to escape the past. Kilburn, the Willesden-adjacent neighborhood where the book is set, is a lively cacophony of contradictions: hope and despair, experience and innocence, poverty and wealth. "Ungentrified, ungentrifiable," Smith writes of Willesden in the novel. "Boom and bust never come here. Here bust is permanent."

Willesden, one of the most diverse areas in London.

To promote the book, Smith's publisher posted a series of short videos on YouTube in which the author read passages over photographs of the places mentioned: Willesden Lane, Camden Clock, 37 Ridley Avenue. One advantage of returning to her own neighborhood, Smith noted at the time, was that she knew the streets: "I don't need to use Google maps; they're kind of a deep knowledge in me."

WHERE TO VISIT

Willesden
London NW6 7TP
UK

Poets' Corner in Westminster Abbey is perhaps the most famous literary landmark in London—a focal point for national pride and a must-visit for the book-minded traveler. Countless authors of international repute—many are still read avidly today, others generally forgotten—have been laid to rest in this section of the eight-hundred-year-old church: Robert Browning, Alfred Lord Tennyson, Charles Dickens, Samuel Johnson, Rudyard Kipling, and Thomas Hardy (though his heart is buried in his local parish church in Dorset), as well as artists in other media, such as the composer George Frideric Handel and the actor Laurence Olivier.

The first poet buried in the Abbey was Geoffrey Chaucer, who died in 1400. He was laid to rest here not because of his literary merits but because he held a high-ranking Crown office overseeing the Palace of Westminster. Nearly two centuries later, the poet and dramatist Edmund Spenser asked to be buried near his literary idol, and the tradition took hold.

Many other writers who were buried elsewhere are commemorated in Poets' Corner by plaques, busts, and ornate monuments. Among them are William Shakespeare, Jane Austen, W. H. Auden, William Blake, the three Brontë sisters, Robert Burns, Lord Byron, Lewis Carroll, George Eliot, Walter Scott, Dylan Thomas, and Oscar Wilde. The plaque honoring novelist Samuel Butler, who died in poverty, speaks up for the many writers not sufficiently appreciated or supported while they were alive who nonetheless are celebrated and immortalized in death:

The poet's fate is here in emblem shown,
He ask'd for bread, and he received a stone.

WHERE TO VISIT

Westminster Abbey
20 Dean's Yard
London SW1P 3PA
UK

Poets' Corner in Westminster Abbey.

Scotland's Enchanted Neverland

Peter Pan, by J. M. Barrie
Dumfries, Scotland

He spends his limitless days cavorting among fairies and mermaids, fighting with pirates, making spur-of-the-moment trips to, let's face it, *abduct* children whose parents have left them at home for the night. He can fly. He will never grow up.

One of the best-loved characters in children's literature, Peter Pan made his first appearance in a few chapters of the writer James Matthew Barrie's 1902 novel, *The Little White Bird*, which he later spun off into a separate book titled *Peter Pan in Kensington Gardens*. In that story, Peter lives among the fairies and other magical creatures in London's famous royal park, where they can move around freely after the gates have closed and the public has left. In 1912, Barrie personally commissioned a statue of his famous creation, surrounded by his creature friends and playing his flute. It stands there to this day. In the 2004 film *Finding Neverland*, Barrie, played by Johnny Depp, gets the idea for Peter Pan and the

Moat Brae, where Barrie first dreamed up Neverland.

The early nineteenth-century mansion is poised to reopen as a children's literary center.

Lost Boys from his time spent with the children of a woman he meets one day while walking in the park.

Yet the Peter Pan story that most readers today are familiar with—thanks to the 1953 Disney film—has its origins elsewhere. Two years after *The Little White Bird* came out, Barrie wrote a play, *Peter Pan, or The Boy Who Wouldn't Grow Up*, in which the boy-hero visits London to whisk Wendy Darling and her two mischievous brothers off to Neverland. The inspiration for that timeless paradise is 350 miles north of London, in Dumfries, a modest-sized market town on the western Scottish coast (which, incidentally, was also home to the eighteenth-century poet Robert Burns).

In 1873, the thirteen-year-old Barrie moved to Dumfries to attend a local academy. He became friends with two boys from the wealthy family that owned Moat Brae, a Greek Revival villa built fifty years earlier on a serene patch of greensward sloping down to the River Nith, a broad vista of hazy hills in the distance. The boys often played games in the gardens of the estate, imagining they were pirates or the survivors of a shipwreck on a distant island. There was even a nearby cave that made for a perfect lair.

In 1924, on his last visit to Dumfries—the author was receiving the ceremonial keys to the town's gates—Barrie said that the years he spent in the area "were probably the happiest of my life, for indeed I have loved this place." He fondly recalled his childhood "escapades" in the Moat Brae garden. It was, as he put it, an "enchanted land," and his and his friends' adventures were "the genesis of that nefarious work—*Peter Pan*."

In the two centuries since it was built for a local lawyer, Moat Brae has passed through many different hands. It served as a residence for most of the nineteenth century and as a nursing home for most of the twentieth. Then it was sold to a developer, who planned to turn the beguiling property into a hotel, but nothing came of the idea. Left to the mercy of vandals, the property fell into disrepair. In 2009, just days before it was scheduled to be demolished, house and land were purchased by a trust specially set up to preserve them. With a little help from the Scottish government and from private donations, the building has been remodeled for the establishment of a National Centre for

Children's Literature and Storytelling, including a library, reading room, performance space, and an apartment for a writer-in-residence. The brand-new Neverland Discovery Garden will include a fairy bower and a pirates' lookout. Peter Pan never wanted to grow up. Neither will Moat Brae.

WHERE TO VISIT

Moat Brae
National Centre for Children's Literature and Storytelling
George Street
Dumfries, Scotland DG1 2EA
UK
https://www.peterpanmoatbrae.org

"When I Die Dublin Will Be Written in My Heart"

Ulysses, by James Joyce
Dublin, Ireland

James Joyce once declared that if the entire city of Dublin "one day suddenly disappeared from the Earth it could be reconstructed out of my book." He was referring, of course, to *Ulysses*, the epic novel set in the Irish capital on

a single day: June 16, 1904. Following two characters, middle-aged carnivore Leopold Bloom and young writer Stephen Dedalus (Joyce's fictional alter ego) as they make their way through the city, each of the twenty-four "episodes" in the novel parallels the parts of Homer's *Odyssey*. (Dedalus is also the protagonist of Joyce's first novel, *A Portrait of the Artist*

Dublin in 1904, the year when *Ulysses* takes place.

as a Young Man, published in 1916.) A landmark work in the development of modern literature, celebrated for its stream-of-consciousness narration, its intricately woven web of symbols, and its faithful representation of the irreducible complexity of daily life, *Ulysses*—published on February 2, Joyce's birthday, in 1922—is also perhaps the most fully place-based work in all of world literature. Forget about virtual-reality headsets: To follow Bloom and Dedalus as they take in the sights and sounds and smells of their city is to be as fully immersed in a time and place from the past as it will ever be possible to be.

Thanks to innumerable books, articles, and readers' guides, it's incredibly easy to see the Dublin sights immortalized in *Ulysses*. In the opening episode, Stephen wakes up at Martello Tower at Sandycove, perched on a coastal promontory south of Dublin. Built a century earlier to watch out for an invasion of Ireland by Napoleon, the tower was later turned into a rented residence; Joyce stayed there with a friend for a few days in 1904, the year in which *Ulysses* takes place. Since 1962, the tower, renamed the James Joyce Tower and Museum, has been open to the public, along with its collection of Joyce-themed memorabilia. Not far away is Sandymount Strand, the expansive beach where Bloom famously masturbates as a flirtatious young lady lifts her skirt and reveals her legs for him; close by, fireworks explode. (This scene, among others, was the reason the book was banned in the United States until 1933.)

A life-sized statue of Joyce striking a pose in the heart of Dublin.

With his adulterous wife, Molly, whose affair with her boss, Blazes Boylan, occupies much of her husband's thoughts in the novel, Bloom lives at No. 7 Eccles Street. He famously begins his day with a breakfast of assorted meats, including "mutton kidneys which gave to his palate a fine tang of faintly scented urine." It's also where, at the end of the novel, Molly makes love to Boylan, as the narration tracks her thoughts in page after page of run-on sentences, finally ending "…and yes I said yes I will Yes." Scandalously, the house was torn down in 1967; a hospital went up in

its place. Fortunately, the front door was saved and later donated to the James Joyce Centre on Great George's Street. Since its opening in 1996 (in an eighteenth-century building that once belonged to a Dubliner mentioned a few times in *Ulysses*), the center has presented exhibits about the author's life and work, as well as lectures and a variety of walking tours organized around themes like "Joyce & the Irish Literary Revival," "*Ulysses* in Sandymount," and a Joyce-themed pub crawl.

Among the stops on that boozy tour is Davy Byrnes, where in the novel Bloom enjoys a lunch of a gorgonzola sandwich and burgundy wine. Both items are still on the menu at this obligatory stop on any walking tour of Joyce's Dublin. Another such place is Sweny's Pharmacy, where Bloom buys lemon-scented soap. No longer a pharmacy, Sweny's sells secondhand books and offers a gathering place for fans of Joyce and literature. Staffed by volunteers, it offers daily readings from Joyce's works.

Any day is a good one for traveling around Dublin scouting the spots from *Ulysses*. But June 16, the date of the action (if that's the right word) in the novel, is when the literary pilgrim, so often pursuing explorations alone, will have the most company. First celebrated in 1954, when the revelers set off to walk from Martello Tower along the route taken by Bloom through the city—they didn't make it; they got too drunk—Bloomsday has since become a citywide carnival, full of turn-of-the-century costumes, pub crawls, musical performances, reenactments, and marathon readings of the entire novel. In recent years the celebration has spread all around the world, from Prague to Montreal, Melbourne to Trieste, Wichita to Worcester. But the most meaningful celebration, of course, takes place where the novel is set. Explaining why hundreds of Dubliners turn out every year dressed as Leopold or Molly, the Irish writer Declan Kiberd once wrote in the *Guardian*: "It is quite impossible to imagine any other masterpiece of modernism having quite such an effect on the life of a city." It is equally impossible to imagine a city having such an effect on an author. "When I die," Joyce once said, "Dublin will be written in my heart."

Davy Byrnes pub, where Leopold Bloom eats lunch.

Martello Tower, where Joyce himself once stayed, and where his fictional alter ego, Stephen Dedalus, wakes up in the first chapter of *Ulysses*.

WHERE TO VISIT

James Joyce Tower and Museum
Sandycove Point
Dun Laoghaire, Dublin A96 FX33
Ireland

http://www.joycetower.ie

James Joyce Centre
35 North Great George's Street
Rotunda
Dublin D01 WK44
Ireland

jamesjoyce.ie

Davy Byrnes
21 Duke Street
Dublin D02 K380
Ireland

https://davybyrnes.com

Sweny's Pharmacy
1 Lincoln Place
Dublin D02 DW26
Ireland

http://www.sweny.ie/site/

Trespasses Sweetly Urged: Places from the Plays

The Tragedies of William Shakespeare
Venice, Italy
Verona, Italy
Helsingør, Denmark
Cawdor, Scotland

Along the Grand Canal in Venice there is a narrow Gothic edifice distinctive for the recurring wheel motif of its intricately carved balconies (unique in the city) and the crest proudly displayed for passing gondoliers and tourists. The crest belongs to the Contarini clan, one of Venice's founding families and some of Italy's oldest nobles.

Those are the facts. The myth, however, is somewhat different: Tradition says the house belonged to Shakespeare's Desdemona, the beautiful Venetian lady murdered by her Moorish husband, Othello, for supposedly betraying him with his lieutenant Cassio. Shakespeare based the plot of his play on a story called "A Moorish Captain," from an Italian volume by the writer Cinthio first published in 1565. Cinthio, in turn, seems to have modeled his tale on the life of Nicola Contarini, of the famous Venetian family, a local leader with skin so dark he was called "the Moor." Like Othello, Contarini led

Desdemona's house in Venice.

troops against the Ottomans early in the sixteenth century. Contarini's story tracks nicely with Shakespeare's, except that rather than strangling his adulterous wife to death in a fit of jealousy, Contarini himself was murdered. His wife, meanwhile, returned to live with her family.

It may seem a thin thread on which to hang a centuries-old tourist attraction, yet still the legend persists—aided by generations of painters and photographers who have depicted the Contarini mansion and called it Desdemona's.

WHERE TO VISIT

Palazzo Contarini Fasan
Calle del Minotto
30124 Venice
Italy

Two households, both alike in dignity,
in fair Verona, where we lay our scene…

So begins *The Most Excellent and Lamentable Tragedie of Romeo and Juliet*, probably Shakespeare's earliest tragedy (scholars date it to the early 1590s). It's one of the Bard's best-loved (and most devastating) plays. But where, exactly, are these dignified homes the opening lines speak of? So true to life has the tale of feuding families and star-crossed lovers felt to nearly five centuries of readers and theatergoers that many have insisted there must be real-world antecedents for the fictional characters, real-world places where they swore love oaths under cloak of night's darkness, lamenting "th' inconstant moon," defying the stars.

So powerful, indeed, has this desire been that, *poof*, just like that, readers' wishes were granted (even if the ill-fated hero's and his heroine's could not be). In 1905, a very special building in Verona went up for sale. Dating to the thirteenth century, it once belonged (as the still-extant coat of arms shows) to the Cappellos, a family of local spice merchants. It has long been suspected that the Cappellos served as the model for the Capulets in Shakespeare's play, which was inspired by Arthur Brooke's *Tragicall Historye of Romeus and Juliet*, published in 1562. Brooke's history was inspired in turn by Italian writers (including Dante) who spoke of a deadly family feud with origins in some forgotten ancient dispute. When the Cappello place hit the market in the early twentieth century, the city of Verona snapped it up and added a Juliet-style balcony to make the claim more plausible.

Today, the house remains open for public tours. Inside, visitors find Renaissance-era costumes and period-style furnishings used in the lavish 1968 film version. Outside there's a statue of Juliet, the right breast

Juliet's famous balcony, in Verona.

rubbed to a shine by visitors hoping for the good luck she never had. Beneath the balcony from which Juliet famously pleaded, "O Romeo, Romeo, wherefore art thou Romeo?" the walls have been covered over with several layers of lovers' signatures and romantic messages, often stuck there with chewing gum. A few years ago the problem got so bad the city banned the practice, on pain of a hefty fine. *O trespass sweetly urged!*

Conveniently, both for that notorious night stalker Romeo and for the modern literary pilgrim, the hearthrob's pad stands a short walk from his beloved's. With even less of an evidentiary basis than the story behind Juliet's house, tradition assigns to her forbidden love the Casa di Cagnolo Nogarola, a thirteenth-century castle-like edifice with high walls, a tower, and a series of courtyards. It once belonged to the Montecchi family—bitter rivals of the Cappellos, or so the story goes—who needed an urban fortress to defend them against their enemies. Apt inscriptions are offered on the exterior walls, like Romeo's heartsick, anguished cry:

> *Tut, I have lost myself. I am not here.*
> *This is not Romeo. He's some other where.*

Unlike Juliet's place, Romeo's house is private, though there is a restaurant on the ground floor that includes some of the original rooms of the house.

WHERE TO VISIT

Juliet's House
Via Cappello, 23
37121 Verona
Italy
https://casadigiulietta.comune.verona.it

Romeo's House (private)
Via Arche Scaligere, 2
37121 Verona
Italy

Sweden—a fine place to look for migratory loons and enemy ships entering the Baltic Sea. With its stone parapets and copper steeples, the castle offers a plausible picture, to the untrained eye, of medieval Scandinavian royal splendor. Yet it wasn't until 1420 that a fort first went up on the site. The structure now there was built not long thereafter (it has since been destroyed and reconstructed) and became a home for Danish kings. It's near the town of Helsingør, commonly anglicized as Elsinore, the fictional home of that most famous and fragile of medieval Danish princes, the ambitious, the ambivalent Hamlet, one and only son of the lately murdered king.

Daunting, forbidding Kronborg Castle is poised at the edge of a peninsula jutting into the strait separating Denmark from

Kronborg Castle, the inspiration for Hamlet's Elsinore.

Experts say Shakespeare's representation of Elsinore in the play is an almost uncannily accurate depiction of Kronborg in real life, even though it's highly unlikely he ever made it to the headquarters of Danish royalty himself. Instead, the Bard probably learned details about the castle from actors who traveled throughout the Continent or from English merchants who had stopped in its bustling port.

Open for tours, Kronborg is full of fascinating sights—like King Frederick II's ornate ballroom—but the main attraction is and always has been its connection to what in some ways is the darkest of Shakespeare's many dark works. For two centuries—the practice began in 1826, to mark the two hundredth anniversary of the Bard's death—*Hamlet* has been performed inside the walls of the castle that serves as its setting; actors from Laurence Olivier in the 1930s to Jude Law in 2009 have played the difficult title role. The tradition continues in less rarefied form as well: All day, as visitors tour the castle, actors perform scenes from the play, and every summer a Shakespeare festival is held on the grounds. For casual visitors, there's a tour that follows in Hamlet's quaking footsteps. Kronborg is easily reached by train from Copenhagen—statues of Hamlet and Ophelia greet visitors at the Helsingør station. In 2000, UNESCO added Kronborg Castle to its list of World Heritage Sites.

WHERE TO VISIT

Kronborg Castle
Kronborg 2 C
3000 Helsingør
Denmark
http://kongeligeslotte.dk/en/palaces-and-gardens/kronborg-castle.html

Shakespeare based *Macbeth*, in some ways the most relatable of his tragic heroes, on King Mac Bethad mac Findlaích, as he was known in the Scots language, who was born around the turn of the second millennium AD. The real Macbeth's career took a dark turn, similar to but slightly different from that of his fictional alter ego: The historical Macbeth killed the king, Duncan, on the battlefield, not in bed, and claimed the throne for himself. His reign lasted seventeen years, not the few weeks of Macbeth's term in the play. He was killed in battle against Duncan's brother and son.

There are many places to visit in Scotland that claim a connection to the play. Glamis Castle is Macbeth's home at the beginning of the action, though it has no connection to the historical figure. The property includes a Macbeth Trail with scenes from the play carved into oak and fir trees.

According to the prophecy of the witches Macbeth encounters in the first scene, he will become the Thane of Cawdor before becoming king—and soon enough Duncan names him to the role. Cawdor Castle still stands strong and imposing in the Scottish Highlands, and might seem like a plausible home for an eleventh-century prince on the rise, but for one notable fact: It wasn't built until three centuries after Macbeth's bloodstained reign. Such chronological niceties didn't bother Shakespeare, however. Incredibly, Cawdor is still owned by the same noble family that inherited it in the sixteenth century; they kindly keep the castle and its lovely grounds open to the public.

Perhaps the best-known place associated with Macbeth is Dunsinane, Duncan's castle in the play and Macbeth's once he murders his way to the throne. In reality, Dunsinane is a bare-faced hill near the town of Perth, with remnants of two medieval forts at the summit. Unfortunately, the ruins were ransacked by relic-seeking nineteenth-century Shakespeare fans, heedless of the fact that the location has no known connection to the historical Macbeth.

Equally famous is "Great Birnam Wood," which the witches say will come to "high Dunsinane hill" and mark the end of Macbeth's ill-gotten reign. Macbeth, of course, thinks he is safe. How can an entire forest travel the fifteen miles that journey would entail? Yet, with a little help from Macduff and his friends, the forest manages the feat. At Birnam Wood today, two trees remain from

The woods of Dunsinane.

Glamis Castle, where Macbeth begins his rise to the throne.

the old forest—an oak and a sycamore—both aging and propped up on crutches. Only the oak is said to date to the real Macbeth's reign, one thousand years ago—though nobody has tested it, and the claim is probably not true. (It is at least five hundred years old, however.) Shakespeare visited the area in 1599 as part of a troupe of comedic actors.

For a site associated with the historical Macbeth, though not mentioned in the play, truly devoted literary travelers can head to Inverness, where the eleventh-century king had his castle. Note, however, that the one now visible in the city was not built until 1836.

Other places in Scotland associated with the homicidal status-climber include the "blasted heath" where Macbeth first encounters the witches, and Lumphanan, where the real Macbeth was executed by his victorious successor Malcolm—the hurly-burly done, the battle lost and won.

WHERE TO VISIT

Glamis Castle
Angus DD8 1RJ
Scotland
UK
https://www.glamis-castle.co.uk

Cawdor Castle
Nairn IV12 5RD
Scotland
UK
https://www.cawdorcastle.com

The spires of the Church of Saint-Jacques in Illiers-Combray.

The Combray Way

In Search of Lost Time, by Marcel Proust
Illiers-Combray, France

In the first pages of Marcel Proust's seven-volume novel, *In Search of Lost Time*, the narrator recalls his difficulty falling asleep when he was a child, particularly at his family's home in the country, in the rural outpost of Combray. He can recall little else of that time until the taste of a madeleine dipped in tea catapults his mind back to childhood, and the whole world of Combray comes alive again. The novel explodes into a cornucopia of aesthetic meditations, endless analyses, and profound reflections on the nature of society, sexuality, art, the self, and, of course, time. The village of Combray and its vicinity are described in intricate, loving detail, from the church steeple that rises above the medieval buildings to two divergent countryside rambles that his family takes for leisurely strolls. In the final volume, the narrator returns to Combray and comes to recognize the falsehood of much of what he had once thought true. He learns, for instance, that the two seemingly irreconcilable paths were connected all along.

Proust's real-life model for Combray was the north-central French village of Illiers, not far from Chartres, where the Proust family had roots going back to the sixteenth century. Proust's family visited Illiers often when the writer was a boy. He loved the landscape, the buildings, the views of the village, the hawthorn trees that bloomed along the paths. The geography of Illiers, its people and its rhythms, became immortalized in one of the most astounding works of fiction ever written.

In 1971, to mark the hundredth anniversary of the author's birth, the village of Illiers added Combray to its name, and the house he used to stay in as a child, and where he hoped more than anything that his mother would come up to give him a good-night kiss, was turned into the Marcel Proust Museum.

WHERE TO VISIT

Marcel Proust Museum–House of Aunt Léonie
6 Rue du Docteur Proust
28120 Illiers-Combray
France

http://www.amisdeproust.fr

Proust's aunt's house, now a museum.

The Breath of Paris: From the Towers to the Sewers

The Novels of Victor Hugo
Paris, France

In addition to being the source material for famous musicals and animated films, Victor Hugo's best-known novels, *Les Misérables* and *The Hunchback of Notre Dame*, were both set in the mid-nineteenth-century Paris that the author lived in and fought to preserve throughout his life. Laced throughout the epic tales of inequality, oppression, redemption, war, and love are depictions of the unparalleled beauty and romanticism of the city's Gothic structures, which Hugo feared were fast disappearing in favor of more modern buildings and conveniences.

Hunchback, Hugo's breakout novel, published in 1831, is set in the medieval center of Paris, known as the Île de la Cité, where both Notre-Dame Cathedral and the Palace of Justice are situated. The novel tells the tragic story (don't let the triumphant Disney version fool you!) about a disfigured bell-ringer named Quasimodo, who is shut away from human society in the cathedral's bell towers by the evil Archdeacon Frollo. Even from his perch atop the city, however, Quasimodo manages to fall in love with a member of Frollo's least favored group of people, the gypsy dancer Esmeralda.

Thanks in part to conservation-minded Parisians like Hugo, visitors can still see Notre-Dame's original bell towers, flying buttresses, and stained-glass windows. In the text, Hugo, an architecture aficionado, celebrates the various features of the cathedral as "harmonious parts of one magnificent whole…a vast symphony in stone."

Nearby is the Palace of Justice, where Frollo brings supposed "criminals" to sequester, torture, and even kill. In the novel's opening pages, Hugo describes throngs of people gathered in the palace yard, below its "lofty Gothic facade," for the Feast of Fools. The masses gave the "appearance of a sea, into which five or six streets, like the mouths of so many rivers, disgorged their living streams." It is here, at the end of the novel, that Quasimodo dies, trying to save Esmeralda from execution. Though the palace has been reincarnated in various forms, one can visit the grand structure, which still has some parts dating from the medieval period.

On a more hopeful note, Hugo's *Les Misérables*—which he took seventeen years to complete before its publication in 1862—tells the story of the escaped convict, Jean Valjean, who turns his life around and adopts a daughter, Cosette. She eventually falls in love with Marius, one of the revolutionaries in the June Rebellion of 1832.

Notre-Dame Cathedral, where Quasimodo is imprisoned by the archdeacon.

When Marius first catches a glimpse of Cosette, she is taking her daily walk with her father in the Jardin du Luxembourg. The tall trees and small nooks where "the sparrows were giving vent to little twitters in the depths of the chestnut trees" are a good place for Marius to remain unseen until he eventually introduces himself.

After meeting Cosette, Marius is wounded at the barricades. Despite the "death on

The museum at Victor Hugo's house devoted to the author's life and work.

every side," Valjean heroically rescues the unconscious Marius and carries him through the fetid sewers, the "secret trapdoor of Paris," back to safety with Cosette. (This part of the novel is titled "The Intestine of the Leviathan.") While it's not possible, even if one wanted to, to crawl into Paris's sewers today, the Paris Sewer Museum chronicles the surprisingly fascinating story of the development of the city's water system from the thirteenth century to the present.

At the end of *Les Mis*, Marius and Cosette are wed in the Church of Saint Paul–Saint Louis in the Marais neighborhood. A real parishioner of the seventeenth-century Jesuit-built Baroque church, Hugo chose to set this triumphant scene here, where people "halted in the Rue Saint-Antoine, in front of

Saint-Paul, to gaze through the windows of the carriage at the orange-flowers quivering on Cosette's head."

There are other places in Paris to connect with Victor Hugo. The writer's home on the second floor of the Hôtel de Rohan-Guéménée, where he lived from 1832 to 1848 with his family and wrote many of his works, is now a museum. Dine at the Grand Vefour in the Palais-Royal, which was frequented by Hugo and other literary elite in the nineteenth century. Today it is a Michelin-starred restaurant, with the original mirrored walls and neoclassical paintings, where you can even request to sit at the author's favorite table. "To breathe Paris," Hugo once said, "is to preserve the soul."

WHERE TO VISIT

Notre-Dame Cathedral
6 Parvis Notre-Dame–Place Jean-Paul II
75004 Paris
France
http://www.notredamedeparis.fr

Palace of Justice
2 boulevard du Palais
75001 Paris
France
http://www.paris-conciergerie.fr/en

Paris Sewer Museum
Face au 93 Quai d'Orsay
75007 Paris
France
http://equipement.paris.fr
/musee-des-egouts-5059

Victor Hugo House
6 place des Vosges
75004 Paris
France
http://www.maisonsvictorhugo.paris.fr/en

Construction of Notre-Dame began in the mid-twelfth century and was finished about one hundred years later.

On the Knight-Errant's Trail in La Mancha

Don Quixote, by Miguel de Cervantes
Consuegra, Spain

A book-addled knight-errant and his plucky squire pal are riding across the dusty, wind-swept plains of La Mancha, searching for down-and-out maidens to rescue from the clutches of various ne'er-do-wells, when thirty-plus long-armed giants appear on the horizon. The knight, Don Quixote, announces with gallant flourish his intention to engage the monsters in battle and destroy them. "It is a great service to God,"

Quixote tells his sidekick, "to wipe such a wicked brood from the face of the earth."

All of which sounds fine to Sancho Panza, but for one minor complication. "What giants?" he asks Quixote.

Digging his spurs into Rocinante, the washed-up steed Quixote has mistaken for a prize stallion, the knight gallops off to battle, advising his alarmed attendant, if he's so scared of the monsters, to "go away and say your prayers, whilst I advance and engage them in fierce and unequal battle."

Unequal, indeed! Quixote plunges in his

The famously monster-like windmills of La Mancha.

A playful statue of Quixote wooing Dulcinea in the fair lady's hometown of El Toboso.

lance, but just then a fierce breeze rises off the plains, swinging a windmill into rapid rotation. The knight and his horse go hurtling across La Mancha's barren ground. Sancho runs to his side, but, courageously, Quixote refuses to admit he is hurt. That's the knight-errant's way.

Though it's only a fleeting episode in Miguel de Cervantes's classic mock-epic from the early seventeenth century, Quixote's ill-fated battle has turned "tilting at windmills" into universally recognized shorthand for the dangerous hallucinations that often accompany delusions of grandeur. Yet for the modern traveler venturing through

Cervantes country in central Spain, it's possible, perhaps, to sympathize with the deceived knight. Dozens of old-fashioned grain-grinding windmills, dating back half a millennium, still dot the countryside, ghostly survivors of a long-vanished world.

Many places in La Mancha market themselves as the inspiration for the famous battle scene, but the hillside town of Consuegra may have the most solid claim, with twelve reconstructed windmills lining a ridge above the town, next to a medieval castle right out of the enchanted landscape from the book. One has been opened as a small museum. Be careful, though: The same heat that heightened the knight-errant's mania hasn't abated in the last four hundred years, so the windmills are best seen in the morning.

Forty miles away is El Toboso, which has a museum in the home of the local woman on whom Cervantes supposedly modeled Dulcinea, Quixote's beloved—but possibly nonexistent—queen. A sculpture in the town square of El Toboso shows the knight-errant kneeling before his queen. Actors sometimes stroll through the square dramatically performing scenes from the book.

Puerto Lapice is the town where Quixote stays at an inn, which he takes to be a castle, and convinces its keeper, whom he presumes to be its lord, to knight him. Venta del Quijote, a restored, white-walled inn, with a small museum of Quixote-inspired illustrations, feels straight out of the time of Cervantes and has a restaurant featuring La Mancha's regional cuisine.

WHERE TO VISIT

Windmills of Consuegra
45700 Consuegra
Spain
http://www.consuegra.es
/conoce-consuegra/monumentos
/molinos-de-viento

Museum-House of Dulcinea del Toboso
Calle Don Quijote, 1
45820 El Toboso
Toledo
Spain
http://www.patrimoniohistoricoclm.es
/museo-casa-de-dulcinea-del-toboso

Venta del Quijote
El Molino, 2
13650 Puerto Lapice
Ciudad Real
Spain

Music and Madness in a Mediterranean Monastery

A Winter in Majorca, by George Sand
Majorca, Spain

In November of 1838, the hottest couple in Paris, cigar-smoking radical feminist Amantine Lucile Aurore Dupin (pen name: George Sand) and the Polish-born composer Frédéric Chopin, boarded a ferry in Barcelona for a winter's vacation on the island of Majorca. Chopin, a lifelong asthmatic, had been having difficulty breathing in the crowded, cloistered city, so he and Sand (and her two children) set off to soak up the Mediterranean warmth and the breezy sea air.

Majorca is lovely in summer but dismal in winter.

At first it was heaven. "The sun shines all day and people are dressed as in the summer-time, because here it is hot," Chopin enthused in a letter from Palma, the Majorcan capital. Sand, too, was taken by the island's pleasant scenes. "The nature, the trees, the sky, the sea, the monuments surpass all my dreams: this is the promised land!" she wrote a friend.

As they moved around the island, however, the weather—and their moods—changed. It was surprisingly cold, rainy, and windy, where they had expected all sunshine and southern heat. Traveling around the island became hazardous: "rains, torrents, swamps, quickset hedges, ditches, all bar the path in vain; one does not stop for such trifles, because, of course they are part of the road. So you are left to contemplate the scenery either in expectation of death or in hope of a miracle."

They began to feel confined on the island. "As the winter advanced, the gloom froze all my attempts at gaiety and calm," Sand later wrote in her memoir, *A Winter in Majorca.* "We felt like prisoners, far from any enlightened help or productive sympathy."

For one thing, they had trouble finding decent lodging. "In a country so close to

The Carthusian Monastery of Valldemossa, where George Sand and Frédéric Chopin briefly lived.

civilized Europe," Sand recalled, "we found it difficult to understand why we were unable to find a single inn…In Palma one has to be recommended and introduced some months ahead to 20 of the more important local personages if one does not want to end up sleeping in the open air." Eventually, they found their way to furnished rooms, but they were in the kind of "disreputable area where a stranger is lucky if he can find a trestle-bed with a mattress a little softer and little more yielding than a slate, a rush chair and food dominated by peppers and garlic." *Peppers and garlic*: the horror!

The couple's problems only worsened when a doctor in Palma diagnosed Chopin with tuberculosis, a disease that to wary Majorcans was only a little less scary than the plague. When their landlord found out, the increasingly unhappy pair was tossed out on the street.

Eventually, they found shelter in a nearly empty Carthusian monastery in Valldemossa, first built as a royal palace in the late four-teenth century, with views of the sea. Their spirits rose. "We are planted between heaven and earth. The clouds cross our garden at their own will and pleasure, and the eagles clamor over our heads," Sand enthused. "It is one of those views that completely over-whelm one, for it leaves nothing to be desired and nothing to the imagination. All that a poet or a painter might dream of, Nature has created here."

Chopin, especially, found inspiration in the atmosphere at the monastery. After a long delay, a piano he had shipped from Paris finally arrived, hauled up the mountain by a team of donkeys. He got to work. What fol-lowed is widely recognized as having been one of the most productive periods in the compos-er's life, during which he produced some of his most delicately haunting pieces. It was here in the Majorcan monastery, for instance, that he composed his renowned twenty-four pre-ludes, including the famous "Raindrop." In *A Winter on Majorca*, Sand described the piece as "full of the drops of rain which resounded on the sonorous tiles of the monastery, trans-formed in his imagination and his music into tears falling from heaven on his heart."

However good for the music, the con-stant downpour was disastrous for the com-poser's health. Holed up in the dismal, drafty monastery, Chopin turned angry and despondent, prone to fits of explosive rage.

Sand later wrote in her autobiography that Chopin thought the place "full of terrors and phantoms, even when he was well."

What made their isolation even worse was that the conservative locals so disap-proved of their unconventional relationship that some refused to even sell them basic goods. The strong-willed Sand, of course, repaid their hospitality in her travelogue by deriding their food and dwellings and call-ing the Majorcans themselves "barbarians" and "monkeys."

The twentieth-century poet Robert Graves, who lived on Majorca and translated Sand's book into English, thought he knew the real reason Sand didn't like the island. According to Graves, Sand's young daughter Solange wasn't fond of her mother's relation-ship with Chopin. One day she decided to play a trick on the sickly composer by dress-ing up as a monk and creeping into his room in the middle of the night. The startled com-poser ran to a priest to seek forgiveness for his sins, which he received—so long as he and Sand ended their illicit relations. Together for another nine years, they never had sex again.

When Chopin's health worsened through the winter, the unhappy little troupe decided to head back to Paris. There wasn't time to arrange to take the piano, so they sold it to a local couple.

These days, fans of both Sand and Chopin flock to the Valldemossa monastery, which

The piano on which Chopin wrote the famous "Raindrop" prelude.

has turned the couple's former rooms into a small museum and includes, as a highlight of the tour, the piano on which Chopin wrote his preludes. Every year the monastery plays host to a Chopin festival. Majorca, of course, has changed quite a bit in the last 180 years. The island has hundreds of fine hotels and great art museums. One tip for the winter literary traveler: Bring a warm coat. It's colder than you might think.

WHERE TO VISIT

The Royal Carthusian Monastery
Plaça de la Cartoixa
07170 Valldemossa
Majorca
Spain

https://www.cartoixadevalldemossa.com/en/

In Search of the True Segovia Bridge

For Whom the Bell Tolls, by Ernest Hemingway
Segovia, Spain

In Ernest Hemingway's *For Whom the Bell Tolls*, published in 1940, the hero, an American teacher of Spanish named Robert Jordan, first glimpses his target through the branches of pine trees perched on a steep hillside. The two-lane steel bridge, Hemingway writes, "spanned, in solid-flung metal grace, a deep gorge," where, "far below, a brook leaped in white water through rocks and boulders."

Jordan is a volunteer with the International Brigades, fighting on the Republican side in the Spanish Civil War. A Soviet military officer advising the rebels has tasked him with blowing up the bridge to prevent the fascists from countering an upcoming Republican offensive. It will be a "very complicated and beautiful operation," the Soviet officer says. It will also be extremely dangerous.

Jordan spends most of the three days the novel covers hiding out with local guerrillas in a cave near the bridge. Among them he

The picturesque Spanish town of Segovia.

The bridge at the center of Hemingway's *For Whom the Bell Tolls* spans a deep gorge somewhere in the Sierra de Guadarrama Mountains.

meets a Spanish woman named Maria, with her "thick short golden hair that rippled as a grain field in the wind on a hillside." Her parents have been brutally killed by the fascists; she has been raped. Despite the horrors of the war, she and Jordan fall in love.

Supplies are scant, and the guerrillas are reluctant to go through with the attack on the bridge. Jordan insists they have to, even if it means sacrificing his own life and the lives of others. The novel ends with the unforgettable final sentence: "He could feel his heart beating against the pine-needle floor of the forest."

In writing his best-selling book about solidarity, sacrifice, and death, Hemingway drew on his own experiences as a reporter in Spain during the Civil War. The book is set high in the Sierra de Guadarrama Mountains, near Segovia, a town known for its gorgeous Roman aqueduct. *For Whom the Bell Tolls* is full of local place names, demonstrating the author's familiarity with the terrain.

Yet it's not easy to figure out where the facts end and the fiction begins. There was indeed a Republican offensive in Segovia in the spring of 1937. Hemingway wasn't in the country, but just a month earlier he had been riding horses in the Guadarrama Mountains with Martha Gellhorn, the war correspondent who would later become his third wife.

As for the bridge itself, there have been conflicting reports about whether it was based on one in reality. In *Papa Hemingway*, a 1966 memoir of his friendship with the Nobel Prize winner, the writer A. E. Hotchner recounts a trip through southern Europe that he took with Hemingway in 1959 (two years before the author took his own life). Together the travelers revisited some of Hemingway's old haunts. One day they stopped by Segovia and took a picnic lunch up into the mountains. According to Hotchner, Hemingway showed off both the cave where the guerrillas supposedly lived and the bridge itself—rebuilt after its destruction—which Hotchner describes as "higher and thicker and more impregnable-looking" than the novel had led him to imagine. He even says they walked together across the bridge.

Forty years later, a British journalist named Richard Barry went searching for the Segovia bridge. A forest ranger he happened to come across gave Barry directions—"north of the Navacerrada pass, crossing Rio de las Lombrices"—and told him it hadn't in fact been blown up during the war, though an attempt had been made. When he got there—glimpsing it, as Hemingway described, through the branches of nearby pines—Barry noticed that the bridge was made of stone, not steel. Hemingway had himself been inconsistent on this point, insisting when the book first came out that his publisher depict a steel bridge on the cover, while later telling Hotchner it was made of stone. It's impossible, therefore, to say conclusively that it is in fact "the real bridge."

Of course, it doesn't matter. At one point in their journey, Hotchner asked Hemingway how much of *For Whom the Bell Tolls* was based on real events. "All good books have one thing in common," Hemingway replied. "[T]hey are truer than if they had really happened."

A deeper level of meaning, a glimpse of what Hemingway found in Segovia, is perhaps best put in another of his works, *Death in the Afternoon*, the nonfiction book about Spanish bullfighting he published in 1932, even before the Spanish Civil War broke out. When you consider everything, including the "fine road to Segovia," that makes Madrid—and, by implication, Spain generally—so special, Hemingway writes, "It makes you feel badly, all questions of immortality aside, to know that you will die and never see it again." He did see it again, of course, in real life, as readers still can in his breathtaking novel.

WHERE TO VISIT

Segovia, Spain
40003

Many pensiones (bed-and-breakfasts) offer rooms with views over the Arno.

Love and Loss in Florence

A Room with a View, by E. M. Forster
Florence, Italy

"It was pleasant to wake up in Florence," E. M. Forster writes early on in his 1908 debut novel, *A Room with a View*; "to open the eyes upon a bright bare room, with a floor of red tiles which look clean though they are not; with a painted ceiling whereon pink griffins and blue amorini sport in a forest of yellow violins and bassoons. It was pleasant, too, to fling wide the windows, pinching the fingers in unfamiliar fastenings,

to lean out into sunshine with beautiful hills and trees and marble churches opposite, and, close below, the Arno, gurgling against the embankment of the road."

Pleasant, indeed! But not everyone has the privilege. Forster's novel concerns an unhappy young Englishwoman named Lucy Honeychurch who is on a visit to Italy with a burdensome older cousin. They take rooms at the Pensione Bertolini in Florence, overlooking the River Arno, but are disappointed to find that both their rooms have views of the garden, rather than the river, the bridges, the hills. A gentleman named Mr. Emerson and his son, George, overhear the ladies complaining about the matter and offer to swap rooms, since they both have river views; the ladies politely decline, in part because the Emersons, simply by making the suggestion, come off a tad sketchy, a bit unrefined.

The heart wants what it wants, however, and after a hot-and-heavy kiss in a field full of violets, Lucy and George are happily married. By the end of the novel, they're back in the Pensione Bertolini, taking in the magical sights and sounds of Florence from their room with a view.

It was in 1901, while on vacation with his mother, that the twenty-two-year-old Forster first visited Florence and stayed at a small hotel on the Lungarno—the road along the Arno waterfront—called the Pensione Simi. They had two rooms, one on the ground floor, and another one floor up—the room with a view. Forster was just starting out as a writer, and soon after arriving in Florence he decided to ditch his stalled first attempt at a novel and start a new one.

There are a few contenders for the claim of serving as Forster's model for the Pensione Bertolini, but the one with the best claim is the

Florence is an enchanting city from any perspective.

building where the Pensione Simi (later called the Pensione Jennings Riccioli) once was—Number 2 Lungarno delle Grazie. It's not an especially satisfying visit, however, for the building has undergone extensive renovations, and now houses several unrelated businesses.

Even one of the characters who stayed in the pensione wasn't able to find it later on. In 1958, Forster added an appendix to a new edition of the novel, bringing the story up to the present day. George and Lucy raised a family, lived through ups and downs, including two world wars. During the second, after George is taken prisoner by the Italian forces in Africa, he finds himself in Florence, and sets off to find the pensione he and Lucy stayed in so many years earlier. "He failed," Forster writes. "For though nothing is damaged all is changed. The houses on that stretch of the Lungarno have been renumbered and remodelled and, as it were, remelted…so

that it is impossible to decide which room was romantic half a century ago."

The 1985 movie version, directed by James Ivory, was filmed in part at the classy four-star Hotel degli Orafi, right on the Arno, which still has some remnants of a thirteenth-century tower on the premises. The hotel's fourth-floor "Room with a View" allows guests "to relive those fascinating, romantic moments and the perfume of a bygone era," the website boasts.

WHERE TO VISIT

Hotel degli Orafi
Lungarno degli Archibusieri, 4
50121 Firenze
Italy
https://www.hoteldegliorafi.it/en/

The Neighborhood That Put Stockholm on the Map

The Millennium Trilogy by Stieg Larsson
Stockholm, Sweden

Stieg Larsson's Millennium trilogy has sold more than eighty million copies around the world, putting the grittier, more diverse side of twenty-first century Stockholm on the literary map. In *The Girl with the Dragon Tattoo*,

The Girl Who Played with Fire, and *The Girl Who Kicked the Hornet's Nest*, investigative journalist Mikael Blomkvist works with expert hacker Lisbeth Salander to look into stories of murder, spycraft, and crimes by and against the state. For the most part the series is set in Sodermalm, an island neighborhood peopled by a diverse array of classes and ethnicities. It

The building where Larsson's stand-in, the journalist Mikael Blomkvist, lives in a penthouse.

has gentrified quickly in the years since Larsson's novels were published, shortly after his sudden death in 2004, and is now hailed as the hippest neighborhood in the city.

With over one hundred of them, Stockholm has more museums per capita than any other city in the world. Among them is the Stockholm City Museum, which since 2008 has offered a popular Millennium Tour of Sodermalm that includes many of the locations from the books. It begins on the old cobblestones outside Bellmansfatan 1, the yellow apartment building atop Mariaberget Hill that is Blomkvist's home. From his sun-soaked attic aerie, with its

Gothic-style spires, the editor looks down on Stockholm's old town, Gamla stan.

Swedes love drinking coffee—they especially cherish the tradition of *fika*, socializing over cups of joe. The tour brings travelers past Mellqvist Kaffebar, the coffee spot preferred by Blomkvist and his creator, Larsson, who often worked there on his laptop. Just upstairs were the offices of *Expo*, the antiracist magazine he founded and edited, and on which Blomkvist's own magazine, *Millennium*, is based. On a nearby corner is the 7-Eleven where Lisbeth Salander often stops to buy frozen pizzas and cigarettes.

Other stops on the walking tour include Adat Jisrael, the Jewish synagogue where the detective Jan Bublanski goes to worship—and to meet with a contact in charge of a private security firm; the public statue called "The Sisters," supposedly based on a reported drowning in the early twentieth century; and the intimate Lebanese restaurant Tabbouli, where Larsson often ate lamb stew and which he used as the inspiration for the Bosnian restaurant in the novels, where a dramatic shoot-out takes place in the final volume.

The last stop on the tour is Lisbeth Salander's posh apartment at Fiskargatan 9, at the top of a building from 1910. The indomitable, black-haired hacker is said to have grown up in a socialist-era working-class apartment building on Lundagatan, but by the second book of the trilogy she has made enough money through her netherworld exploits to buy a sprawling penthouse of twenty-one rooms. She only bothers to furnish three of them. The sign on the door says V. KULLA, a reference to the villa of that other famous Swedish literary heroine, Pippi Longstocking, a model for Larsson in creating the older character of Salander. A reconstruction of Longstocking's villa can be visited at a children's park on Stockholm's Djurgarden Island.

The café where Blomkvist often works.

Sodermalm, the island neighborhood where the Millennium series is set.

WHERE TO VISIT

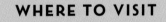

Stockholm City Museum
Ryssgarden
116 46 Stockholm
Sweden

https://stadsmuseet.stockholm.se

Mellqvist Kaffebar
Rörstrandsgatan 4
113 40 Stockholm
Sweden

Lisbeth Salander's Apartment
Fiskargatan 9
116 20 Stockholm
Sweden

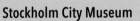

A Steep, Steady Climb to Revelation

The Magic Mountain, by Thomas Mann
Davos, Switzerland

In 1912, the German writer Thomas Mann visited the Swiss mountain town of Davos, where his wife, Katia, stricken with acute bronchitis, was staying in a sanatorium.

Author of an acclaimed 1901 multigenerational family epic, *Buddenbrooks*, Mann had just finished a novella, *Death in Venice*, and was beginning to think about his next project. He found inspiration in the natural beauty of Davos, the mountaintop health institutions, and the winsome sufferers who

The view from the Hotel Schatzalp, a sanatorium left over from the old days.

sought refuge there. He put it all, and much more, into *The Magic Mountain*, now acclaimed as a masterwork of twentieth-century fiction. He didn't think many people would read it, however, and was astonished when the "odd entertainment" became his best-known book. Five years after it was published in 1924, he won the Nobel Prize in Literature.

The novel tells the story of an aspiring

engineer named Hans Castorp, who, as the book opens, is riding in a train to the Swiss mountain village of Davos, up "a steep and steady climb that seems never to come to an end." He is traveling there to visit his cousin, a patient at the International Sanatorium Berghof, perched fifteen hundred meters above sea level. The building, as Mann describes it, has "so many balconies that from a distance it looked porous, like a sponge."

On those balconies, with their south-facing view of a glistening lake, towering firs, and snowy mountaintops, Castorp encounters a colorful group of patients suffering from debilitating lung conditions. They are there to take in the fresh mountain air. Wrapped in camel-hair blankets, they spend their days imbibing sumptuous feasts of chicken and crayfish, followed by ice cream and pastries, soaking up the sun's rays, and breathing the air whose purifying effects many in Davos compare favorably with the pleasures of drinking champagne. The patients edge closer to death but maintain a sense of humor and a dynamic approach to life that Castorp finds invigorating. Those who are sick seem, in many ways, to be healthier than those who are not.

The days at the sanatorium, Mann writes in *The Magic Mountain*, soon become something of a blur, "a continuous present, an identity, and everlastingness." Castorp means to stay for just three weeks, but he

Davos is now better known for the World Economic Forum than as a resort for curing tuberculosis.

doesn't leave for another seven years, long after his cousin has already gone home.

Ill and ailing people have been visiting Davos from all around the world since the 1860s, when a German doctor noticed that nobody who lived there suffered from tuberculosis, unlike the many thousands of Europeans who died from the disease every year. Well-off guests paid for food and lodging. It was a thriving business: At one time there were as many as forty sanatoriums in Davos. But in the 1940s, the discovery of penicillin threw the institutions into crisis. With tuberculosis all but cured, the target clientele shifted to asthmatics. Most sanatoriums closed or were converted into ski-friendly hotels.

Davos has changed, and traces of the vanished world from *The Magic Mountain* are somewhat hard to find. Mann apparently based the interior scenes on the Waldsanatorium, where his wife stayed, but that structure was rebuilt in the 1950s, and looks nothing like it did in his day. The exterior of the Berghof was probably based on the Sanatorium Valbella. Opened in 1898, it managed to stay in business until 2004, one of the last health institutions remaining in the village. It finally closed when German insurance companies, pinching pennies, balked at paying to send patients to the Swiss mountaintop resorts. "Our problem is that sick people are no longer being sent to Davos," the town's mayor told the *Guardian* newspaper at the time the Valbella closed. "The air is still wonderful, though. In the morning it is fresh and cool. The climate is exhilarating."

Exhilarating, indeed, and not only for the sick and the dying—also for the rich and famous. After the sanatoriums closed up shop in the second half of the twentieth century, Davos became known for its world-class skiing and, more recently, for the annual World Economic Forum, put on every January for the amusement of glad-handing politicians, plutocrats, pundits, princes, and other plunderers—visiting lords and ladies of what Mann, from the vantage point of the magic mountain, called "the catastrophe-smitten flat-land," the fallen world below.

Perhaps the best-preserved vestige from Mann's time in Davos is the Hotel Schatzalp, the only sanatorium mentioned by its real name in *The Magic Mountain*. High in the sky, it looks much the same as it would have a century ago—down to the balconies where patients used to lie out in the sun. The most recent proprietor told a *New Yorker* reporter in 2014, "Maybe our luck here is that, at the time when everybody renovated the old buildings, they didn't have money to renovate the Schatzalp." Something living and meaningful and deep has emerged in a place once neglected and left for dead—a perfect echo of Thomas Mann's story.

WHERE TO VISIT

Hotel Schatzalp
Promenade 65
7270 Davos Platz
Switzerland
https://www.schatzalp.ch/en/

An Awakening at Austerlitz

War and Peace, by Leo Tolstoy
Austerlitz, Czech Republic

The Battle of Austerlitz, in 1805, involved some 150,000 combatants. One-sixth of them did not leave the battlefield alive— anonymous victims of history's deadly march. Perhaps the greatest victory of Napoleon's nearly twenty-year romp across Europe, it was a disastrous rout for the Allies trying to keep him hemmed in, especially for the Russian and Austrian

Historical reenactments are a common sight at the Austerlitz battlefield.

forces leading the anti-French coalition at the time.

A devastating memory in the Russian imagination, it was also an irresistible subject for Leo Tolstoy, whose epic novel set during the Napoleonic Wars, *War and Peace*, was originally titled, somewhat less epically, *The Year 1805*. The Battle of Austerlitz

comes at a pivotal point in the book, at the end of the first volume, and Tolstoy's treatment of it is classic: panoramic in its sweep, describing in detail the troop movements across the vast landscape, yet intimate in its approach to the individual fates playing out amid it all—the solitary men left to bear the brunt of the surge toward French victory.

One of those men Tolstoy zooms in on is Prince Andrei, one of the main characters in the book. Bored with domestic life and ignored by his pregnant wife, the dashing Andrei decides to join the army—even though he will be sent to fight the troops of Napoleon, his idol. He is among the many thousands at Austerlitz. At the decisive moment of the battle, as his fellow soldiers fall all around him, Andrei bravely seizes the regimental flag and rallies his men toward the fighting. He hears "with delight the whistle of bullets, evidently aimed precisely at him," Tolstoy writes. Soon, before he, too, is cut down.

Wounded, Andrei lies on the ground under a "quiet, peaceful, and solemn" sky. Questioning what it's all for—the guns and the gore—he realizes that it's meaningless and vain. "Everything is empty, everything is deception," Andrei concludes, "except that infinite sky." It is possible for him to be happy.

Even when he wakes up to find Napoleon, who saves him from dying on the battlefield, Andrei can only think back to what he saw in "that lofty, equitable, benevolent sky," and the "solemn and sublime train of thought which weakness, loss of blood, suffering, and the nearness of death" had induced in him. "Looking into Napoleon's eyes," Tolstoy writes, "Prince Andrei thought of the insignificance of greatness, the unimportance of life, which no one could understand, and of the still greater unimportance of death, the meaning of which no living person could understand and explain."

The sprawling Austerlitz battlefield lies fifteen miles east of the Czech city of Brno, where package tours are offered to visit the two-century-old killing fields. A peace monument erected in 1915 pays homage to the dead, and the chateau where the truce ending the battle was signed is available for tours. No memorial, however, credits the writer who pointed out what all the carnage added up to: nothing.

WHERE TO VISIT

Austerlitz Battlefield
602 00 Brno
Czech Republic
https://www.austerlitz-battlefield.com

A towering peace memorial in honor of the seventeen thousand lives lost in the battle.

Two museums in the same Moscow apartment building compete to tell the story of Mikhail Bulgakov and his beguiling novel.

An Evil Apartment in Moscow

The Master and Margarita, by Mikhail Bulgakov
Moscow, Russia

It's early in the Soviet era when the devil and his minions arrive in Moscow, set up headquarters in a communal apartment building, host a lavish ball, and plunge the city into chaos.

Mikhail Bulgakov's maniacally mystical novel, *The Master and Margarita*, has been a cult classic since it was first published in the late 1960s—first in a censored version in a Russian magazine, and then in full as a book in Paris. For years, the work existed in Russia only in the form of the suppressed, underground literature known as *samizdat*. The authorities believed, perhaps rightly, that a work of such caustic, pointed satire and brimming with such a wry take on humanity might be a threat to their regime.

In 1921, soon after the Revolution, the Kiev-born Bulgakov moved into the

building he would later use for many of the scenes in *The Master and Margarita*. Once full of luxury rentals, the turn-of-the-century Art Nouveau structure was later turned into one of the first communal apartment buildings in Moscow—several families split a single flat, one to a room. While Bulgakov and his wife lived in the apartment, they shared it with sixteen other people, including a baker, a salesman, and a typesetter. The aspiring author hated the arrangement, writing a poem at the time:

> *On Bolshaya Sadovaya street*
> *Stands a great block of apartments*
> *In the block live our brothers in evil:*
> *The organized proletariat*
> *And I was engulfed by the proletariat,*
> *As if I was an atom (sorry for the*
>   *comparison)*

The building was turned into one of the first collective residences after the Russian Revolution.

Our facilities are really lousy
Nothing works…
The sink goes its own way too
Dry during the day, and at night it flows
  on to the floor

Partly because he disliked communal living, and partly because he wanted to take up with another woman, Bulgakov moved out of the building in 1925. But when, three

years later, he began work on his masterpiece, he used it as the book's setting.

Bulgakov worked on the novel through the height of the Stalinist terror, until 1940, when he died. Once he had to rewrite it from memory a year after burning the only copy he had.

Even though the novel was suppressed in the Soviet Union—or, more likely, because of that—Bulgakov's old apartment building on Bolshaya Sadovaya became a gathering place for the Moscow counterculture, a common place of pilgrimage for artists and hippies inspired by the darkly comic novel. The walls beside the staircase leading to the author's former lodgings, the "Evil Apartment" from his book, became covered in graffiti inspired by the novel—quotes from the text, sketches of the characters. There was a constant battle between the young pilgrims and the authorities, who tried to obliterate the graffiti, ultimately with little success.

Today, the graffiti remains, but the situation at the building is complicated: There are two competing museums, both devoted to the legacy of Bulgakov and the setting of his best-known work. The one on the ground floor, called the Bulgakov House, opened in 2004 and boasts a collection of materials related to the author's life, a full library of Bulgakov-related works, and even a 1930s-style tearoom. It also offers regular walking tours of the Moscow sites mentioned in the book, including the nearby Patriarch's Ponds, where the opening scene takes place. (A sign at the spot jokingly warns against speaking with strangers—a winking homage to the novel.) Bulgakov is still controversial, however, and some of the property belonging to this independent museum was vandalized in 2006 by a crank who thought Bulgakov's work was satanic—which, in a sense, the best sense, it is.

Upstairs, in the author's old apartment, is a separate museum supported by the Moscow government. Even today, it seems, the Russian authorities are eager to maintain some control over this potentially dangerous work. The M. A. Bulgakov Museum shows what the communal apartment looked like in the author's time and plays host to cultural events like jazz and classical performances, theater, and discussion clubs. Oddly, it claims to be "the only and first Memorial Museum of Mikhail Bulgakov,"

which anyone with their eyes open on entering the building knows is incorrect. Culture-industry pretensions and bureaucratic absurdities, it seems, have outlasted the regime Bulgakov so wickedly satirized in *The Master and Margarita*. The time may yet come for the devil to return.

WHERE TO VISIT

Bulgakov House
10 Bolshaya Sadovaya Street
125047 Moscow
Russia

http://dombulgakova.ru

M. A. Bulgakov Museum
10 Bolshaya Sadovaya Street
Apartment 50, Floor 4, Entrance 6
125047 Moscow
Russia

http://bulgakovmuseum.ru/en/

A Murder in St. Petersburg

Crime and Punishment, by Fyodor Dostoevsky
St. Petersburg, Russia

Amid a searing heat wave in St. Petersburg, a poor, disheveled, confused student makes a fateful decision: He will murder an elderly woman in cold blood. He will do it quickly and he will not get caught. He will see how much the fate of one mean, unlovable old woman really matters.

Fyodor Dostoevsky's *Crime and Punishment* shows the grim street life of a poor neighborhood in St. Petersburg, full of drunks, brawlers, and prostitutes. The action mostly takes place in a fairly confined area of the city that can easily be covered in a short walk.

The opening scene describes Raskolnikov leaving his apartment on a street only called S. Place, where he lives in a dingy, cramped room "of a most miserable appearance, with dusty, yellowish wallpaper peeling off the walls," and walking slowly "towards K. bridge." Dostoevsky hid the place names in order to get around the imperial censors, but the real locations used as models for the book are easy to figure out. "S. Place" refers to Stolyarni

Lane, often translated as Carpenters Lane, while the bridge is Kokushkin bridge over the Griboedov Canal. The canal-front is a pleasant, tree-lined walk, but in Dostoevsky's day it was a grimy, seedy, polluted waterway that helped make St. Petersburg a notoriously unsanitary city, rife with illness.

It's simple enough these days to follow Raskolnikov around the relatively small area covered by most of the book's action. He lived at 5 Stolyarni Lane. A sculpture of him, made in 1999, stands out in relief from the corner of the building, showing the emaciated criminal descending the narrow staircase. An accompanying plaque says in Russian:

The building where, in *Crime and Punishment*, the impoverished student Raskolnikov rents a dusty, closet-sized room.

THE TRAGIC FATES OF THE PEOPLE

OF THIS PART OF PETERSBURG

SERVED

DOSTOEVSKY

AS THE BASIS FOR HIS PASSIONATE SERMONS

ON GOOD FOR ALL HUMANKIND

The St. Petersburg of Dostoevsky's time was overcrowded with serfs emancipated by the czar in 1861. In the book, the author describes poverty-stricken Sennaya Square, generally translated as the Haymarket, St. Petersburg's version of Skid Row, where the lower classes, the down and out, tend to congregate. It's there that Raskolnikov decides to commit his senseless crime.

Dostoevsky's St. Petersburg is almost a completely different city from the imperial capital of grand palaces and opulent balls depicted in Alexander Pushkin's *Eugene Onegin*, published shortly before Dostoevsky got to town. "Rag pickers and costermongers [fruit-sellers] of all kinds were crowding round the taverns in the dirty and stinking courtyards of the Hay Market," Dostoevsky writes. "Raskolnikov particularly liked this place and the neighboring alleys, when he wandered aimlessly in the streets." The street-level taverns in the square "were all swarming with various sorts of merchants and ragamuffins."

Sennaya Square has changed quite a bit in the century and a half since Dostoevsky wrote *Crime and Punishment*. Once dominated by a massive church, later destroyed by the Soviets to make way for a metro station, today there's only one building left from Dostoevsky's time: a yellow-fronted police station known as the Guardhouse, where the author was actually locked up for violating censorship codes in the 1870s. He used his time behind bars to read *Les Misérables* by Victor Hugo.

The old woman Raskolnikov decides to kill lives in a building supposedly based on one on the canal's waterfront, at 104 or, alternatively, 15 Srednyaya Podyacheskaya—it has a front and back entrance. Raskolnikov creeps up the narrow staircase three times: first to go on a trial run for the murder, then to commit the act, and later out of an inexplicable impulse to revisit the scene of his dastardly crime.

The author knew well the neighborhood he was writing about so intimately. Born in Moscow, he was sent to live in St. Petersburg when he was sixteen years old, after his mother died of tuberculosis. He would end up living in more than twenty different places in the city throughout his life. From 1864 to 1867, while he worked on *Crime and Punishment*, Dostoevsky lived on a second-floor apartment in a building on the corner of Raskolnikov's own Stolyarni

The apartment–now a museum–where Dostoevsky once lived.

Lane. There's a plaque on the building noting that fact.

Elsewhere, an apartment Dostoevsky lived in both as a young man and again for the last three years of his life (that was where he finished *The Brothers Karamazov*, and where he died) has been turned into a museum devoted to the author's life and work. An old grandfather clock is frozen at the hour and minute of his death. The museum, which opened in 1971, is usually a stop on any number of walking tours offered of Dostoevsky's St. Petersburg. The author is buried in Tikhvin Cemetery at the Alexander Nevsky Monastery, in another part of town.

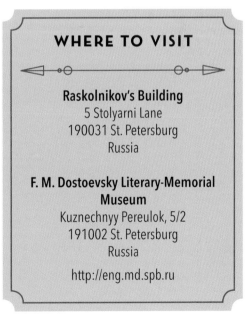

WHERE TO VISIT

Raskolnikov's Building
5 Stolyarni Lane
190031 St. Petersburg
Russia

F. M. Dostoevsky Literary-Memorial Museum
Kuznechnyy Pereulok, 5/2
191002 St. Petersburg
Russia

http://eng.md.spb.ru

ASIA & OCEANIA

Desire and Obsession in Istanbul

The Museum of Innocence, by Orhan Pamuk
Istanbul, Turkey

Kemal, the narrator in Nobel Prize laureate Orhan Pamuk's enthralling 2008 novel, *The* *Museum of Innocence*, is a wealthy business-man in 1970s Istanbul. Engaged to one woman, he falls madly in love with another—a beautiful but poor shopgirl named Fusun, a distant relative. They commence a torrid

The Museum of Innocence is a tribute to obsession and the transcendent nature of the trivial.

but short-lived affair. When, after attending his engagement party, Fusun disappears, Kemal calls off the wedding and begins to rummage through the fast-changing city—with its "familiar Istanbul smell of sea and moss, pigeon droppings, coal smoke, car exhaust and linden blossoms"—for any trace of his vanished lover.

Years later, she has remarried. Kemal cozies up to her dopey husband, a filmmaker, and dangles the prospect of financing his next movie. The proximity to Fusun is torture, but it has its compensations. For nearly a decade, through stints of blissful, illicit lovemaking and painful separation, Kemal obsessively collects objects with even the barest connection to their deep but impossible bond: earrings, discarded olive pits, perfume bottles, old postcards, a tricycle, lottery tickets, thousands of cigarette butts, panties. His nostalgia—for a life with his lover he never got to live, for Istanbul's rich but quickly vanishing past—is so manic that after Fusun's death he buys her family's house and turns it into a museum for his collection of Fusun-related memorabilia. "Istanbul," Kemal says, "was now a galaxy of signs that reminded me of her."

In 2012, Pamuk opened the doors of a

The museum, opened by Pamuk in 2012, offers an intriguing portal between the worlds of reality and fiction.

real-life Museum of Innocence on a backstreet in the city's newly trendy Cihangir neighborhood. Situated in a narrow, red, Ottoman-era building, among winding alleys and old antique shops, the museum, ostensibly a presentation of Kemal's collection from the novel, is in fact made up of various items Pamuk collected while he worked on the book. The ground-floor exhibit is a display case of 4,213 cigarettes that Fusun once smoked. Other rooms on higher floors contain audio recordings from Istanbul in the twentieth century, as well as photographs, paintings, and manuscripts of the novel. There are eighty-three glass cases, one for each chapter in the book. Pamuk conceived of the museum and the novel as complementary parts of the same project; at the end of each copy of the novel is a free ticket to the museum. The effect is a blurring of the boundaries between fact and fiction, imagination and reality—not unlike the experience of obsession itself.

"A museum should not be flags—signs and symbols of power—but intimate works of art," Pamuk once told an interviewer. "It should express the spirituality of the collector." The Museum of Innocence certainly reflects Pamuk's, as well as the philosophy laid down by his forlorn narrator, who explains near the end of the book his reason for collecting: "to teach not just the Turkish people but all the people of the world to take pride in the lives they live."

WHERE TO VISIT

Museum of Innocence
Cukurcuma Street, Dalgic Cikmazi, 2
34425 Beyoglu
İstanbul, Turkey
https://masumiyetmuzesi-en.myshopio.com

A Wild Garden in Kerala, India

The God of Small Things, by Arundhati Roy
Kerala, India

Arundhati Roy grew up in the southern Indian state of Kerala. Dotted by sleepy backwater fishing villages connected by pristine rivers and streams, the shore lined with swaying palm trees, Kerala is perhaps best seen by taking a tour on the traditional-style thatched-roof houseboats that are popular with tourists.

Roy used Kerala as the setting of her first novel, the Booker Prize–winning *The God of Small Things* (1997), a semi-autobiographical account of family drama, political turmoil,

Kerala, often seen by boat, is a land caught in a web of class conflict and political tension.

and forbidden love. For the devoted literary traveler there are a few sites connected with the book that can be visited. The author has said the Hotel Sealord in Ernakulam was the inspiration for the Hotel Sea Queen of the novel, where the twins Rahel and Estha stay with their mother, uncle, and great-aunt, picking up their ill-fated British-born cousin from the airport. Roy's mother's home is the basis for the family's house in the book. "The old house on the hill wore its steep, gabled roof pulled over its ears like a low hat," Roy writes. "The wild, overgrown garden was full of the whisper and scurry of small lives."

In 2016, an Indian blogger named Mayank Austen Soofi made a pilgrimage to the dilapidated, abandoned house. Some townspeople in Kerala, Soofi reported, consider Roy a disgrace for having written a book that embarrassed her family.

A committed activist for the rights of indigenous peoples and against globalization, Roy spent the years after her novel's publication focused exclusively on nonfiction, publicly excoriating India's shift to a nuclear power and the damming of rural rivers. (She even went to jail for her efforts—for a day.) Not until twenty years after *The God of Small Things* did Roy return to fiction, with 2017's *The Ministry of Utmost Happiness*, set largely in Delhi and Kashmir.

WHERE TO VISIT

Hotel Sealord
Shanmugham Road, Marine Drive
Ernakulam
682031 Kerala
India
http://www.sealordhotels.com

The characters in Roy's first novel stay at the Hotel Sea Queen, modeled after the waterfront Hotel Sealord in Kerala.

Last-Minute Escape at the Saigon Airport

The Sympathizer, by Viet Thanh Nguyen
Ho Chi Minh City, Vietnam

Viet Thanh Nguyen's beguiling novel, a winner of the Pulitzer Prize, opens in April 1975 as Saigon, the capital of South Vietnam, is about to fall to the northern communists. Our narrator is a "man of two minds," and in two ways: He is half-French, half-Vietnamese, and

he is secretly a communist agent working on the staff of a South Vietnamese general. As the general prepares to flee to America, the narrator's handlers have ordered him to go, too, so as to keep tabs on whatever resistance movement the general tries to stir up from afar.

First, however, he has to get his man out of Saigon. With the whole place collapsing before the communist assault, that is no easy

The Sympathizer's conflicted protagonist makes a hair-thin escape from Saigon's Tan Son Nhat International Airport as the North Vietnamese army closes in.

angry that, unlike the privileged elites on the plane, they won't be making it out of the city.

Miraculously, another plane arrives and the refugees sprint toward its open portal, clambering over one another to get inside the last plane leaving the airport, the last leaving Saigon, as the communists close in.

In his own life, Nguyen's escape from Saigon was hardly less dramatic. With his mother and older brother (his father somehow got separated from them), the author was among the crowd thronging the airport that day in April 1975. Unlike the narrator in *The Sympathizer*, the family did not make it onto a plane. They did, however, find their way to a barge, where they happened to run into Nguyen's father, and eventually the family made it to America. Saigon, of course, was renamed Ho Chi Minh City. In 2004, United Airlines sent the first American commercial flight to Tan Son Nhat International Airport in almost thirty years, since the evacuation.

task. After bribing their way into Tan Son Nhat International Airport, the general, his wife, the narrator, and dozens of others, tightly packed together, finally manage to make it on a plane. It's taxiing down the runway when a huge explosion rocks the aircraft: It's under fire, either from communist forces in the outlying suburbs—the narrator's own comrades—or from South Vietnamese troops

WHERE TO VISIT

Tan Son Nhat International Airport
Truong Son, Phuong 2
Tan Binh
741039 Ho Chi Minh City
Vietnam
https://www.hochiminhcityairport.com

A Life-Changing Encounter on a Kyoto Bridge

Memoirs of a Geisha, by Arthur Golden
Kyoto, Japan

As a nine-year-old girl, Chiyo is taken from her family and sold into servitude at a house for geishas in Kyoto. The resident geisha takes a disliking to her, envisioning Chiyo as a potential future rival, and does everything possible to make her life miserable. Broken and bereft, Chiyo collapses in misery one day as she crosses a footbridge over the Shirakawa Canal in Kyoto. A high-society gentleman, known to her as the Chairman, passes by and takes pity on her—the first person in the world ever to do so—and Chiyo decides she will exert all her will to become a famous geisha and deserving of the Chairman's esteem. The encounter on the bridge is the pivotal moment of her life. She learns flower arrangements and makeup and musical instruments and tea ceremonies. Every moment of her performance has to be perfect. Before long Chiyo is the most famous and most beloved geisha in all of Japan.

Thanks in large part to the 2005 film version of *Memoirs of a Geisha*, based on the 1997 novel by Arthur Golden, Tatsumi Bashi, the largest bridge over the canal, has become

Tatsumi Bashi, the pedestrian bridge in Kyoto, where Chiyo first draws the attention of the Chairman.

a popular tourist destination in Gion, the old town of the city, with cobbled streets, overhanging trees, and distinctive orange lanterns. (The film was not shot on location in Kyoto, but on sets in southern California.) Hundreds of geishas still live and work as performers, entertainers, and (purely platonic) escorts in Gion. Maikos, geisha apprentices, dance at the Kyoto Museum of Traditional Crafts. Unfortunately, many travelers make themselves obnoxious pests by attempting to take pictures of geishas passing in cabs or on the street. Pro tip: Put away the camera, enjoy it for what it is.

WHERE TO VISIT

Tatsumi Bridge
Hanamikojidori Shimbashi Nishi Iru
Higashiyama-ku
Kyoto 605-0000
Kyoto Prefecture
Japan

Leaving Thoughts of the World Behind

The Narrow Road to the North, by Matsuo Basho
Tohoku, Japan

Matsuo Basho was a seventeenth-century literary star. A prolific poet in the city of Edo, now known as Tokyo, Basho was a celebrity on the collaborative haiku circuit, the poetry-slam scene of its time and place.

As he got on in years, however, Basho decided to give up his busy cultural life and hit the road on trips throughout the Japanese countryside, taking less-traveled paths, visiting Mount Fuji and the imperial capital at Kyoto. Travel for Basho was a metaphor for life, and necessary to produce the state of *karumi* (lightness) that he found conducive to producing his art.

In the spring of 1689, Basho sold his hut and left on his longest trip yet. "I seemed to be possessed by the spirits of wanderlust, and they all but deprived me of my senses," he would recall in the famous opening passage of his masterwork, *Oku no Hosomishi (The Narrow Road to the Deep North)*, a prose-and-poetry travelogue of the half-year, fifteen-hundred-mile trip. "The guardian spirits of the road beckoned." He wanted to see the sights that poets of centuries earlier had written about; he was himself following in the footsteps of a twelfth-century poet named Saigyo, and sought to visit every location Saigyo mentioned in his works. He was especially eager, he wrote, to see the moon rise in the night sky above the pine-studded islands of Matsushima, off Honshu's northeastern coast.

With a student named Kawai Sora, Basho took footpaths through the hills of Tohoku. Traveling was dangerous, for the sojourners were always at risk of assault by bears and bandits. But the scenic and spiritual rewards were incredible, as immortalized in Basho's classic work. In the shrine-filled city of Nikko, the pair stopped to take in the Urami-no-taki waterfall:

> *For a little while I listen to the sound of*
> *the water,*
> *Hidden behind the waterfall,*

Leaving all thoughts of the outside world
behind,
I feel as though I am at the
Start of a summer retreat.

When he arrived at Matsushima—one of the famous Three Views of Japan—the sight was too much even for his evocative skills. "No person could wield paintbrush or pen to describe this masterful work of the gods," Basho wrote.

The travelers then continued down along the coast of the Sea of Japan to the city of Ogaki. The coastal stretch was the most difficult and strenuous part of the trip. "It was

A footpath at the Yamadera Temple on Mount Hoju.

An iconic red bridge at the Matsushima archipelago.

every man for himself," Basho recalled. Today, there are statues of Basho and Sora standing along the banks of the Mogami River in Yamagata prefecture. When the poet visited the mouth of the river at sunset, he was moved to record the view:

The river Mogami
Has drowned the hot, summer sun
And sunk it in the sea!

For more than three hundred years, travelers have followed in Basho's footsteps, seeking the same simplicity and proximity to nature that drove him to hit the road. There are many ways to experience Basho's narrow road, from throwing a copy of *The Narrow Road* in a rucksack and heading out on the well-maintained coastal trails to options more refined: A company called Walk Japan offers a guided ten-day group tour along Basho's route. There's even an annual commemorative walk in Basho's honor through the remote Natagiri Pass. The price of admission includes lunch and the use of a pair of Basho-era straw shoes.

Ultimately, it doesn't matter how, or where, one travels the narrow road so long as one does. "Every day is a journey," Basho wrote in his immortal work, "and the journey itself home."

In Tokyo, near the bank of the Sumida River, where Basho lived in his thatched cottage, the Basho Museum features Japanese-language exhibits related to the poet and to the haiku culture from which he emerged. Outside are a small garden, a replica of Basho's hut, a statue of the writer, and a fish pond.

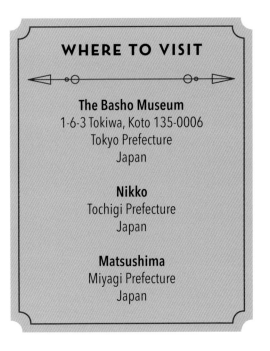

WHERE TO VISIT

The Basho Museum
1-6-3 Tokiwa, Koto 135-0006
Tokyo Prefecture
Japan

Nikko
Tochigi Prefecture
Japan

Matsushima
Miyagi Prefecture
Japan

In Tokyo, a Portal to Another World

The Novels of Haruki Murakami
Tokyo, Japan

On a sunny afternoon in April 1978, a twenty-nine-year-old man, the owner of a struggling café/jazz club, relaxed with a cold beer at a baseball stadium in Tokyo. His favorite team, the Yakult Swallows, was facing off against the Hiroshima Carp. First batter up for the Swallows was a young American ballplayer named Dave Hilton, who promptly doubled into left field and, unbeknownst to him, launched one of the greatest writing careers of the last half-century. "The satisfying crack when the bat met the ball resounded throughout Jingu Stadium," Haruki Murakami later recalled. "Scattered applause rose around me. In that instant, for no reason and on no grounds whatsoever, the thought suddenly struck me: *I think I can write a novel.*"

The novel he then produced, *Hear the Wind Sing* (1979), about a student's return to the city of Kobe, the author's hometown, was the first in what has now become thirteen (and counting) works of long fiction, as well as several other collections of short stories and essays. Murakami is one of the most

Waseda University, where the author studied drama as an undergraduate.

Rokujigen, a café and bookstore devoted to Murakami.

celebrated writers in the world and a peren-
nial contender for the Nobel Prize. Travelers
from all over the world flock to Japan, and
especially to Tokyo, to see some of the places
that figure in his work, including the exciting
(like Jingu Stadium, the second-oldest in
Japan, where Babe Ruth once played) and
the banal (like Metropolitan Expressway
No. 3, where it passes through the Sangenjaya
neighborhood, from which, in Murakami's
dystopian novel *IQ84*, published in 2010, the
main character Aomame, stuck in a traffic

jam, clambers down an emergency escape
and into another dimension of reality).

Other Murakami-related spots in Tokyo
include Waseda University, where the writer
studied (as did Toru Watanabe, the main
character in 1987's *Norwegian Wood*), and
The Old Blind Cat, a jazz club near Shinjuku
Station that he frequented when he was in
college. The café he and his wife owned in
the 1970s, Peter Cat, was located first in the
western suburb of Kokubunji and later in
the more central Sendagaya neighborhood.

In Ogikubo, there's a café, bookstore, and art gallery named Rokujigen, a tribute to Murakami and a gathering place for his fans.

Ken Lawrence, a longtime Tokyo resident and author of a helpful book called *The Murakami Pilgrimage*, hosts a website of the same name that's loaded with details about the real places featured in Murakami's fiction. One post offers a handy guide to "Six Cherry Blossom Spots from Murakami's Novels."

WHERE TO VISIT

Rokujigen Books & Gallery
2F, 1-10-3 Kamiogi
Suginami-ku,Tokyo
167-0043
Japan
http://www.6jigen.com

A Maori Legend from the New Zealand Coast

The Whale Rider, by Witi Ihimaera
Whangara, New Zealand

Witi Ihimaera's 1987 novel *The Whale Rider* tells the story of Kahu Paikea Apirana, a bold young Maori girl who dreams of becoming the chief of her tribe. Set in the remote village of Whangara on the eastern New Zealand coast, the story is a marvelous tale of the upending of communal tradition and the importance of female empowerment. Pai, as the girl is known, is a descendant of Paikea, the legendary man who rode on the back of a whale and led his people to New Zealand. Her ancestry fulfills one requirement for the job of chief, but never before has a woman held the position. Her grandfather is the current chief; her father, an artist living in Germany, wants no part of it. But Pai's grandfather doesn't want to pass the leadership on to her because she is not a boy.

Pai uses tricks and natural abilities to pass all the tests for the job. Unlike the boys vying for the position, Pai finds the whalebone that signifies she is destined for leadership in the tribe. When several whales beach themselves near Pai's home, she climbs atop the back of one to urge it back out to sea—it goes, with her riding on its back. Seeing this, Pai's grandfather finally designates her the next leader of the tribe.

Ihimaera, the first published Maori novelist, based the story on the legend of the people who live in Whangara. (His mother is from the village.) But he wrote the story while living in New York—inspired, strangely enough, by the sight of a whale beached on the banks of the Hudson River.

The village of Whangara, on the New Zealand coast, is caught between the pressure of progress and the tug of tradition.

In 2003, the book was turned into an award-winning movie, filmed on location in Whangara, with locals serving as extras.

Home to only a few dozen people, Whangara is out of the way for any literary pilgrim, even in that isolated part of the world. Situated a few miles off the Pacific Coast Highway on New Zealand's North Island, the village sits on a bay with a small whale-shaped island in the center. Its remoteness, however, hasn't stopped fans of the book and the movie from venturing to the

its capacity to handle them; tourists wandered into places they should not have gone. Still, the village remained open to the world, rather than closed off. As a village elder told a British journalist, "The point is not just to make money. It's to unify. To say, 'Hey, here we are. Come and see us.' It's a beautiful little place."

WHERE TO VISIT

Whangara Marae
Pa Road RD 3
Whangara, Gisborne 4073
New Zealand

The local meetinghouse features a sculpture on its roof of the legend that inspired *The Whale Rider*.

village. In the center of Whangara is Whitireia, the intricately carved community center (or *marae*) built in 1939. Atop the building is a wood sculpture of Paikea riding a whale. After the film came out in 2003, Whangara saw an influx of visitors beyond

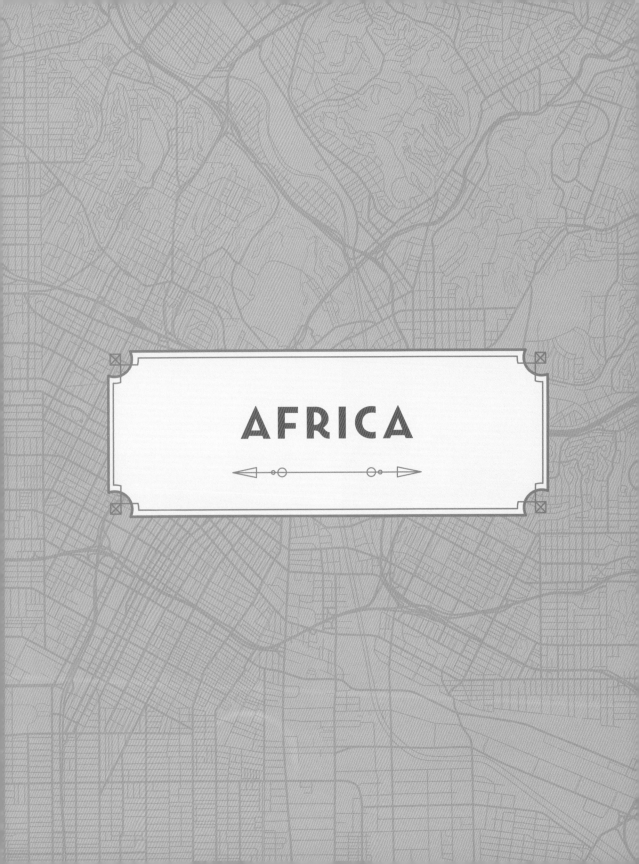

AFRICA

A Revelation at the Harare Sports Club

Martha Quest, by Doris Lessing
Harare, Zimbabwe

Born in Persia to British parents who relocated to Southern Rhodesia (now Zimbabwe) a few years later, Doris Lessing was raised on a farm in the cloistered, confusing confines of race-based European imperialism. After moving to the Rhodesian capital, then known as Salisbury (now Harare), at the age of eighteen, Lessing married and gave birth to two children before the union ended in divorce. In *Martha Quest* (1952), the first installment of Lessing's semi-autobiographical *Children of Violence* series of novels, the heroine spends much of her free time at the segregated restaurant of the Sports Club, a cricket stadium built in 1900 (and still standing, right across from Zimbabwe's presidential palace), where she first notices the underlying tensions of Rhodesian life: The patrons are white, the waiters black. At Sports Club parties, where she drinks too much and dances with ugly fools, Martha receives a world-class education in the shifty ways of colonial society and of its wolflike men. "They did not understand, they understood nothing, they were barbarians," Lessing writes.

The venue also played a pivotal role in the author's own life. In her 1994 autobiography, *Under My Skin*, Lessing recalls the moment, just after World War II broke out

As a young woman, Lessing attended parties on the verandah of the Salisbury Sports Club, now known as the Harare Sports Club.

The club was founded by English colonizers in 1900 as a private polo field.

in Europe, when she realized she would be a writer: "The verandah of the Sports Club was scattered with bitter men," those too old or ill to be accepted into the British army, Lessing recalls with one hand drawing a cigarette to her lips and the other rocking a carriage, forward and back. The men on the verandah, their fears and foibles and frustrations, seemed to offer volumes of material. "I was feeling that pleasure, almost an exaltation, which is how a writer may recognize that her life is matching her natural disposition—her talents," the future Nobel laureate recalled. "I had written very

little then. But I was listening, selecting—*recognizing*." It was a few years after that revelation on the Sports Club verandah that Lessing decided to leave two young children with her husband and set off for London to pursue a literary career.

WHERE TO VISIT

Harare Sports Club
Harare 04-263
Zimbabwe

The Dickens of the Souk

The Cairo Trilogy by Naguib Mahfouz
Cairo, Egypt

In 1988, the Egyptian novelist Naguib Mahfouz became the first—and still the only—Arab-language writer to win the Nobel Prize in Literature. Mahfouz, who died in 2006, is best known for his Cairo trilogy. The novels follow several generations of a single family in Egypt from the revolution against Britain after World War I up to the 1950s. It's largely set in the El-Gamaleya section of Cairo, which dates back to medieval times, where Mahfouz was born. Full of arches, balconies, alleys, and minarets, the neighborhood also boasts the pungent cornucopia that is the Khan el-Khalili souk.

Mahfouz's Cairo novels are full of rich descriptions of life in the city at mid-century. For good reason the writer's exploration of his city has been compared to Charles Dickens's evocations of nineteenth-century London. This, for example, is how Mahfouz, in *Palace of Desire*, the second volume of the trilogy, describes the neighborhood of his youth: "Voices were blended and

In Mahfouz's fiction, the Gamaleya neighborhood of Cairo is both steeped in Islamic history and full of the sights and sounds of contemporary life.

The Mosque of Al-Hussein, where the Prophet Muhammad's grandson's head is buried.

intermingled in a tumultuous swirl around which eddied laughter, shots, the squeaking of doors and windows, piano and accordion music, rollicking handclaps, a policeman's bark, braying, grunts, coughs of hashish addicts and screams of drunkards, anonymous calls for help, raps of a stick, and singing by individuals and groups."

Many of the places mentioned in the Cairo trilogy can still be visited and appreciated today. In the first volume, a woman named Amina, who was married at fourteen and has spent the subsequent twenty-five years locked up inside the apartment she shares with her angry, absent husband, looks out on her sliver of the world, taking in the view of nearby minarets at the ancient madrassas of Barquq and Qala'un. "It was a view that had grown on her over a quarter of a century," Mahfouz writes. "She never tired of it. The view had been a companion for her in solitude and a friend in her loneliness during a long period when she was deprived of friends and companions before her children were born, when for most of the day and night she had been the sole occupant of this large house with its two stories of spacious rooms with high ceilings, its dusty courtyard and deep well."

Later in the novel, Amina briefly escapes from home with her children and visits the Mosque of Al-Hussein, where the Prophet's grandson's head is supposedly buried. The experience moves her to tears: "How often she had longed to visit this site, as though yearning for a dream that could never be achieved on this earth."

Down the block from the mosque, literary travelers can stop for a rest at Naguib Mahfouz Café, where the author used to drink tea, write, and people-watch. As with many writers, cafés were important to Mahfouz: As a child he was introduced to the magic of storytelling by a bard in the coffeehouse next to his parents' home. Later, much of his literary and political education came through arguments in the city's cafés. Other spots associated with Mahfouz in Cairo include Café Riche, where he held weekly salons with other intellectuals, starting in the early 1960s; Qushtumur, which he used for the name of his final novel; and the now-touristy Fishawi Café, where he wrote parts of the trilogy while holed up in the backroom.

"Everyone has a place in time and space," Mahfouz once wrote, "everyone has a point of departure for which he longs and adopts as a refuge, to go back in times of difficulties or when he is away from it. My place is in old Cairo, in al-Gamaliya. My soul is there always, in spite of the passing of long years."

WHERE TO VISIT

Mosque of Al-Hussein
36 Al-Mashhad Al-Husseini
El-Gamaleya
Qism El-Gamaleya, Cairo
Egypt

Naguib Mahfouz Café
El-Gamaleya
Qism El-Gamaleya, Cairo
Egypt

In the late twentieth century, Bowles became synonymous with Tangier in a way rare for a writer not actually from the place he or she wrote about.

Tangier, the Dream City

The Sheltering Sky, by Paul Bowles
Tangier, Morocco

"I've always wanted to get as far as possible from the place where I was born," the writer Paul Bowles once told an interviewer. "Far both geographically and spiritually. To leave it behind. One belongs to the whole world, not just one part of it."

Son of a middle-class family in Queens, New York, born in 1910, Bowles couldn't have gotten much further, spiritually and geographically, from the place of his birth than the old city of Tangier. After dropping out of college, he sailed for Paris, and followed Gertrude Stein's advice to check out the bustling, polyglot city across the Strait of Gibraltar from Spain. He first went there with his friend, the composer Aaron Copland, in 1931. After working as a composer in Paris and New York, he turned once again to fiction, his first artistic pursuit, and received a contract for a novel. With that in hand, he returned to Tangier in 1947; his wife, Jane, also an accomplished writer, joined him the following year.

Apart from winters spent on a private island he owned off the coast of Sri Lanka,

Bowles lived in Tangier until his death in 1999. It's hard to think of a writer so closely associated with a city on a continent he wasn't from. Bowles once called Tangier "a dream city…[with] the classical dream equipment of tunnels, ramparts, ruins, dungeons, and cliffs…a doll's metropolis."

Bowles used Morocco as the setting for his deep and disturbing existentialist novel of 1949, *The Sheltering Sky*. He began working on the novel in the city of Fez, fueled by *kif*, or hashish, and *majoun* (a jam made from cannabis), and then continued to finish it while traveling through the dry desert interior of the area then known as French North Africa.

A small museum devoted to Bowles in the historic building of the Tangier American Legation.

The book tells the story of Port and Kit's travels in the Algerian desert, along with a friend, Tunner, and their descent into death and madness. They think the trip will bring them together but it only tears them apart. *The Sheltering Sky* was rejected as too autobiographical by Doubleday, his first publisher, and it isn't hard to find traces of Bowles and his wife in the two main characters, Port and Kit. "He did not think of himself as a tourist; he was a traveler," Bowles writes of Port. "Whereas the tourist generally hurries back home at the end of a few weeks or months, the traveler, belonging no more to one place than the next, moves slowly, over periods of years, from one part of the earth to another."

Bowles, however, stayed in Tangier, and he was often visited by fellow writers from the United States, like Tennessee Williams, Truman Capote (who called Tangier "that ragamuffin city"), Jean Genet, Gore Vidal, William S. Burroughs (who wrote most of *Naked Lunch* in Tangier), and Allen Ginsberg. His influence on American writers of the mid- to late twentieth century can hardly be overstated. "Paul Bowles opened the world of Hip," Norman Mailer wrote in *Advertisements for Myself* (1959). "He let in the murder, the drugs, the death of the Square…the call of the orgy, the end of civilization."

In 1990, *The Sheltering Sky* brought Bowles a burst of late-life attention when it was turned into a film by Bernardo Bertolucci (the director of Marlon Brando's 1972 film *Last Tango in Paris*), starring John Malkovich as Port and Debra Winger as Kit, with a brief cameo by the author himself.

Having first established himself as a composer, Bowles was enchanted by the music of Morocco, priceless samples of which he recorded for the Library of Congress in what he described as "a fight against time"—more precisely against the rush of modernization that threatened to wipe out Morocco's vibrant folk culture after it earned independence from France in 1956.

Bowles died in his Tangier apartment in 1991, but literary pilgrims still journey to the city to, as one commenter on the travel website Lonely Planet puts it, "bow to the sanctuary!" His haunts aren't that easy to find; nothing in Tangier is. "If you want to be taken to his home now," a journalist wrote in *Vogue* in 2014, "the destination is synonymous with the half syllables of his name; simply direct any driver 'Pa Bo.'" That may be, but there are a few different places you might end up. Bowles lived in several parts of the city over the years, most notably a house named El Foolk on the Old Mountain Road in Sidi Masmoudi, a thirty-acre spread with views of the Strait of Gibraltar, and in the apartment where he died, in Immeuble Itesa, a surprisingly unlovely concrete apartment building near the city center.

To mark the centennial of the author's birth in 2010, the Tangier American Legation opened a special wing to honor Bowles's connection to the city. Its three rooms contain books, photographs, letters, musical scores, suitcases, and other ephemera related to Bowles's life and work. The building, in the old Jewish quarter of Tangier, is a destination in itself: Gifted to the United States by the local sultan in 1821, it is the oldest diplomatic property still in the federal government's possession.

The most important place related to Bowles's work is not in Tangier and cannot be visited in any literal sense. Tennessee Williams put it best in his *New York Times* review of *The Sheltering Sky*: Bowles's work, he wrote, "contains a mirror of what is most terrifying and cryptic within the Sahara of moral nihilism, into which the race of man now seems to be wandering blindly."

WHERE TO VISIT

Tangier American Legation Institute for Moroccan Studies
8 Rue d'Amerique
Tangier
Morocco
http://legation.ipower.com/blog

Mma Ramotswe's Gaborone

The No. 1 Ladies' Detective Agency, by
Alexander McCall Smith
Gaborone, Botswana

While most visitors to Botswana only check out the scenic national parks in the northern part of the country, the last twenty years have brought a new wave of tourists to the capital city of Gaborone. They come not to get a glimpse of exotic animals but to track down locations featured in a series of beguiling and beloved books. In 1998, the Zimbabwe-born Scottish writer Alexander McCall Smith published *The No. 1 Ladies' Detective Agency*, the first of what have become eighteen novels. At first the book garnered little attention or acclaim. Within a few years, however, the series had sold millions of copies and had been translated into many languages.

McCall Smith, who spent time in Botswana before writing the books, has said that the characters and places in the series are a mixture of the real and the fictional. Most memorable of all his creations, of

The rural village of Mochudi, where the indomitable Mma Ramotswe grew up.

Gaborone, the capital of Botswana.

course, is Mma Precious Ramotswe, the big-hearted protagonist who uses money inherited from her father to move to Gabarone and open a private detective agency. Along with her assistant, Grace Makutsi, Ramotswe spends her days riding around the city in a white van, tracking down clues and trying to solve cases: helping people find missing loved ones, helping people free themselves from scams, helping people make up for past mistakes—that is to say, helping people.

There are several places in Gaborone to visit related to Mma Ramotswe. There's her home on Zebra Way (not Zebra Drive, as in the books). There's her favorite store, the Botswana Book Centre, which can be found at the 1960s-era African Mall, a market that also has stands selling her favorite snack: deep-fried mopani worms, washed down with red-bush tea. Forty-five minutes away there is Mochudi, the traditional village where Ramotswe grew up. It was here, while visiting with some friends, that McCall Smith was inspired to write the novels. The village is little more than a cluster of houses of the kind she might have grown up in, with thatched

roofs and mud walls; on a hill overlooking the town is the school Ramotswe would have attended as a child—now a museum devoted to the local Bakgatla culture.

All these and more are stops on various Ladies' Detective Agency tours offered by companies in Gaborone. The guides know their stuff. As Ramotswe's late father says in the first book in the series, "Every man has a map in his heart of his own country and...the heart will never allow you to forget this map."

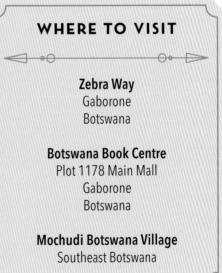

WHERE TO VISIT

Zebra Way
Gaborone
Botswana

Botswana Book Centre
Plot 1178 Main Mall
Gaborone
Botswana

Mochudi Botswana Village
Southeast Botswana

PHOTO CREDITS

page 1 David Wilson/Flickr, **page 2** Russ2009/Flickr, **page 4** James Kirkikis/Shutterstock.com, **page 5** liran finzi sokolovski/Shutterstock.com, **page 7** Zach Frank/Shutterstock.com, **page 8** (top) Zach Frank/Shutterstock.com, (bottom) Erika J. Mitchell/Shutterstock.com, **page 10** Rolf Müller/CC BY-SA 3.0, **page 11** Cindy Hopkins/Alamy Stock Photo, **page 12** Daniel Case/CC BY-SA 3.0, **page 15** Felix Lipov/Shutterstock.com, **page 16** Nagel Photography/Shutterstock.com, **page 18** By EQRoy/Shutterstock.com, **page 19** Gigi Altarejos/EyeEm/Getty Images, **page 21** Courtesy of Newark Public Library, **page 22** Courtesy of Bernhard Ellefsen, **page 23** Courtesy of Richard Kreitner, **page 25** Roman Babakin/Shutterstock.com, **page 28** Jim.henderson [CC0], from Wikimedia Commons, **pages 28–29** Ryan DeBerardinis/Shutterstock.com, **page 30** Allison Meier/flickr, **page 31** Amanda Davis/Flickr/CC BY 2.0, **page 33** Courtesy of Natasja Schouterden, **pages 34** Felix Lipov/Shutterstock.com, **page 35** Courtesy of Andrew Kunkel, **page 37** Brightgalrs/Wikimedia Commons/CC BY-SA 4.0, **page 38** A Samson/Shutterstock.com, **page 40** Courtesy of Bonnie Beebe, Beebe Ranch, **page 41** Michael Ventura/Alamy Stock Photo, **page 42** Courtesy of Atlanta History Center, **page 43** (top) Courtesy of Clayton County CVB, (bottom) Courtesy of City of Marietta, **page 46** Rolf_52/Shutterstock.com, **page 47** Joe Vogan/Alamy Stock Photo, **page 49** Andrea Wright/Flickr/CC BY 2.0, **page 50** mauritius images GmbH/Alamy Stock Photo, **page 51** Courtesy of Penelope Hines; Executive Director of the Monroeville/Monroe County Chamber of Commerce, **page 53** Valis55/Wikimedia Commons/CC BY-SA 3.0, **page 57** © The Historic New Orleans Collection 2010, **page 58** Kimberly Vardeman/Flickr/CC BY 2.0, **page 60** travelview/Shutterstock.com, **page 61** DigitalVues/Alamy Stock Photo, **page 62** Photo by Marit & Toomas Hinnosaar, **page 63** Courtesy of Backspace Bar & Kitchen, **page 63** Courtesy of Hotel Monteleone, **page 64** Don Smetzer/Alamy Stock Photo, **page 65** Courtesy of Nebraska Tourism, **page 67** Jeff Roberson/Kansas City Star/TNS via Getty Images, **page 71** dmac/Alamy Stock Photo, **page 72** Todd Strand/Alamy Stock Photo, **page 74** Laurent DUPONT/CC BY-SA 3.0, **page 76** Martin Shields/Alamy Stock Photo, **page 78** Courtesy of National Park Service, **page 79** 4kclips/Shutterstock.com, **page 81** Randall J Hodges/Getty Images, **page 82** National Geographic Creative/Alamy Stock Photo, **page 86** Steve Wood/Shutterstock.com, **page 87** Courtesy of Mark Gunn, **page 89** jejim/Shutterstock.com, **page 90** Ken Wolter/Shutterstock.com, **page 91** EQRoy/Shutterstock.com, **page 93** Michael Urmann/Shutterstock.com, **page 94** Kent Kanouse/CC BY-NC 2.0, **page 96** Yuriy Chertok/Shutterstock.com, **page 98** Jane Rix/Shutterstock.com, **page 99** Andrews Jebasingh/Shutterstock.com, **page 102** Pictureguy/Shutterstock.com, **page 103** intoit/Shutterstock.com, **page 104** MARGRIT HIRSCH/Shutterstock.com, **page 106** Alice Munro Garden, **page 108** Kuryanovich Tatsiana, **page 109** Roberto Michel, **page 111** Keith Dannemiller/Alamy Stock Photo, **page 112** © Bhupinder Singh, **page 114** Gail Johnson/Shutterstock.com, **page 117** Alastair Wallace, **page 118** Alastair Wallace, **page 120** © The Imperial Torquay, **page 121** (top) Bahadir Yeniceri/Shutterstock.com, (bottom) SADLERC1/Shutterstock.com, **page 122** Nicholas Peter Gavin Davies/Shutterstock.com, **page 124** The History Collection/Alamy Stock Photo, **page 126** steved_np3/Shutterstock.com, **page 128** matthi/Shutterstock.com, **page 131** Greg Balfour Evans/Alamy Stock Photo, **page 133** pxl.store/Shutterstock.com, **page 134** Benjamin B./Shutterstock.com, **page 135** pio3/Shutterstock.com, **page 137** IR Stone/Shutterstock.com, **page 138** Benedictus/Shutterstock.com, **page 140** Jonathan Goldberg/Alamy Stock Photo, **page 141** James Brittain-VIEW/Alamy Stock Photo, **pages 142, 143** Peter Pan Moat Brae Trust/Graeme Robertson, **page 145** Library of Congress, Prints & Photographs Division, LC-DIG-ggbain-21817, **page 146** abd/Shutterstock.com, **page 147** Design Pics Inc/Alamy Stock Photo, **page 148** FLPA/Alamy Stock Photo, **page 149** Barabanschikow Alexander/Shutterstock.com, **page 151** Luca Lorenzelli/Shutterstock.com, **page 152** Jon Nordstrøm/VisitDenmark, **page 154** Bill Anderson/Flickr, **page 155** Francesco Dazzi/Shutterstock.com, **page 156** Oxxo/Wikimedia Commons/CC BY-SA 3.0, **page 157** AGB Photo Library Produções Fotograficas Ltda/Alamy Stock Photo, **page 159** Ttstudio/Shutterstock.com, **page 160** Pack-Shot/Shutterstock.com, **page 161** JeniFoto/Shutterstock.com, **page 162** Yasonya/Shutterstock.com, **page 163** Migel/Shutterstock.com, **pages 165, 168** Medartmed/Dreamstime.com, **page 166** Aldorado10/Dreamstime.com, **page 169** Izabela23/Shutterstock.com, **page 170** Raul Ortega/Shutterstock.com, **page 172** S.Tatiana/Shutterstock.com, **page 173** Sergey Novikov/Shutterstock.com, **page 175** Erik G Svensson/mediabank.visitstockholm.com, **page 176** simon leigh/Alamy Stock Photo, **page 177** Oleksiy Mark/Shutterstock.com, **page 179** Remo Loher/EyeEm/Getty Images, **page 180** Jon Sparks/Alamy Stock Photo, **page 182** Oskar Orsag/Shutterstock.com, **page 184** Richard Sevcik/Shutterstock.com, **page 185** Nikolay Sachkov/Shutterstock.com, **page 186** Anton_Ivanov/Shutterstock.com, **page 189** © A.Savin, Wikimedia Commons, **page 190** Davide Mauro/CC BY-SA 4.0, **pages 193, 194** Innocence Foundation/Refik Anadol, **page 196** DR Travel Photo and Video/Shutterstock.com, **page 197** Sealord Group of Hotels, **page 198** Quang nguyen vinh/Shutterstock.com, **page 200** Stuart Black/robertharding/Getty Images, **page 202** Jochen Schlenker/Getty Images, **page 203** Patryk Kosmider/Shutterstock.com, **page 205** Hitoshi Iyatomi/Shutterstock.com, **page 206** Courtesy of Rokujigen, **page 208** Michael Schwab/Getty Images, **page 209** GlobalTravelPro/Shutterstock.com, **page 211** Hamish Blair/Getty Images, **page 212** Graham Chadwick/Getty Images, **page 213** eFesenko/Shutterstock.com, **page 214** Egyptian Studio/Shutterstock.com, **page 216** imageimage/Alamy Stock Photo, **page 217** Evannovostro/Shutterstock.com, **page 219** Universal Images Group North America LLC/DeAgostini/Alamy Stock Photo, **page 220** Vadim Nefedoff/Shutterstock.com

INDEX

RICHARD KREITNER is a contributing writer at *The Nation* magazine. His work on politics, history, and literature has also appeared in *Slate*, *The Baffler*, and *The Boston Globe*. A lover of books and travel, he is the author of "The Obsessively-Detailed Map of American Literature's Most Epic Road Trip," featured in *Atlas Obscura* in 2015. He lives in Brooklyn, New York.
http://richardkreitner.com @RichardKreitner